GCSE ENGLISH
FOR EDEXCEL

SERIES EDITOR: Peter Ellison

ANDREW LIDDLE

RICHARD ORMROD

SHIRLEY ORMROD

Hodder & Stoughton

A MEMBER OF THE HODDER HEADLINE GROUP

Acknowledgements:

The authors and publishers would like to thank the following for their kind permission to reproduce copyright material:

Copyright Text:
p84–85 extract from a travel website © Igluvillas.com; p90 extract from 'The Other Side of the Dale' by Gervase Phinn, (Michael Joseph, 1988) © Gervase Phinn, 1988; p154 and p189 'My god, it's like New York all over again' by Richard Owen from *The Times*, Friday April 19 2002, © Times Newspapers Limited, 2002; p154 and p170 'Loaded-on-Sea' by Sara Nathan from *The Sun*, April 9, 2002 © News International Newspapers Limited, London, 2002; p155 and p172 'A Mockery of Justice' by Davis Williams and Tom Rawstone from the *Daily Mail*, May 15 2002, © Atlantic Syndication; p158 'Red card for bully dads who tell kids to cheat' by Adrian Lee from the *Daily Express*, April 29, 2002 © Express Newspapers 2002; p162 'I'm Lloyd Webbher' by James Scott from the *Daily Mirror*, Monday, April 29, 2002 © Mirror Syndication International; p163 headline and short extract from the *Daily Telegraph*, Tuesday April 9, 2002; p164 short extracts from the *Daily Mail*, April 11, 2002, the *Daily Express*, April 13, 2002, the *Kent and Sussex Courier*, April 12, 2002, the *Daily Telegraph*, April 12, 2002 and *The Times*, April 13, 2002; p165 'Five-hour rescue for stage that leapt 80ft from cliff' by Michael Fleet from *The Daily Telegraph*, April 23, 2002; p173 'The Tower and the Glory' by Nick Lester from *Plymouth Evening Herald*, October 4, 2001. Reproduced by courtesy of *Plymouth Evening Herald*; p174 Sail Training Association leaflet, used with the kind permission of The Sail Training Association, UK's largest Tall Ships Youth Charity; p176 webpage from the RNIB website entitled 'Understanding retinal detachment' © RNIB; 'Dynamic Tiger Freestyle Kickboxing' leaflet © Mark Griffiths; p178 Newquay Zoo leaflet © Newquay Zoo; p179 South Tynedale Railway leaflet © South Tynedale Preservation Society; p184 'Hey, good looking' by Emma Parker Bowles from Tatler, June 2002 © Tatler/The Condé Nast Publications Ltd; p185 'Need a Lift? from Condé Nast Traveller, July, 2002 © Steve Woods © Condé Nast Traveller/The Condé Nast Publications Ltd; p187 front cover of *Daily Express*, Friday April 19 2002 © Express Newspapers; p195 'Should the Death Penalty be Restored?', POLICE Magazine, 1986, published by the Police Federation of England & Wales; p196 'Capital Punishment for Terrorists?', NACRO; p201–202 extract from *The Blue Peter Green Book* by Lewis Bronze, Nick Heathcote and Peter Brown, reproduced with the permission of BBC Worldwide Limited. Copyright © Lewis Bronze, Nick Heathcote and Peter Brown; p203 'Regimen: Kelly Smith, 23 Footballer, England's women's team' by Nick Wyke from *The Times Magazine*, 11 May 2002.© Nick Wyke/Times Newspapers Limited, 2002; p209 © www.spiceuk.com; p215 extract from *Chinese Cinderella* © Adeliune Yen Mah; p218 extract from *Diamonds are Forever* by Ian Fleming, Glid Rose Publications Ltd 1956. Extract reproduced with permission of Ian Fleming Publications Ltd; p219 extract from *Unicorn Summer* by Rhona Martin © Rhona Martin. Used with permission of the author; p222 advertisement for a Subaru Legacy Estate 2.0 Sport © Subaru (UK) Ltd.; p224 'Has your faith in the crown been restored?' from the Mirror Mailbox, Thursday, April 11, 2002 © Mirror Syndication International; p226 'Jolly good return to an age that never was' by Benedict Nightingale from *The Times*, May 1, 2002 © Times Newspaper Limited, 2002; p227 'Pop, New to Q' by Lisa Verrico from *The Times*, May 1, 2002 © Lisa Verrico/Times Newspaper Limited, 2002; p229 © www.news.bbc.co.uk; p230 'Notable Blunders' from The Times Educational Supplement, April 4, 2002 © Stephanie Northen/Times Educational Supplement, 2002; Droeshout engraving of William Shakespeare, from the First Folio, 1623.

Acknowledgements for Copyright Photographs and Artwork on page iv.

Orders: please contact Bookpoint Ltd, 130 Milton Park, Abingdon, Oxon OX14 4SB. Telephone: (44) 01235 827720. Fax: (44) 01235 400454. Lines are open from 9.00–6.00, Monday to Saturday, with a 24 hour message answering service. You can also order through our website: www.hodderheadline.co.uk

British Library Cataloguing in Publication Data
A catalogue record for this title is available from the British Library

ISBN 0 340 85745 5

First published 2002
Impression number   10 9 8 7 6 5 4 3 2
Year   2008 2007 2006 2005 2004 2003

Copyright © 2002 Andrew Liddle, Shirley Ormrod, Richard Ormrod

Typeset by Fakenham Photosetting Limited, Fakenham, Norfolk.
Printed in Italy for Hodder & Stoughton Educational, a division of Hodder Headline, 338 Euston Road, London NW1 3BH.

CONTENTS

INTRODUCTION

Welcome to *GCSE English for Edexcel*! This coursebook is designed to enable you to get the most out of your GCSE English course. It guides you through the reading, writing and speaking and listening elements of the course, providing a range of activities and advice to help you to achieve your best.

Although this book concentrates on the Edexcel GCSE English specifications A and B, you will see that the Shakespeare and Poetry units also provide coursework assignments and exam preparation suitable for the Edexcel GCSE English Literature specification.

Each unit begins with an explanation of the assessment objectives that apply to each particular element of the specification. These may seem strange at first but they are an important key to success. The assessment objectives tell you exactly what you need to understand and do in order to achieve a good grade. They are what the examiners use to mark your work, and so they give you the opportunity to ensure that you provide what they want to see.

To the teacher

The aim of *GCSE English for Edexcel* is to support every aspect of the Edexcel GCSE English specifications and, when used in conjunction with *GCSE English for Edexcel: Teacher's Resource*, to cover a large proportion of the Edexcel GCSE English Literature specification as well.

As all experienced GCSE English teachers know, one of the trickiest aspects of the current requirements is to integrate the various aspects of the course so that students feel that they are undertaking a coherent course of study. *GCSE English for Edexcel* has been written with this very much in mind. 'Speaking and Listening' and 'Writing to Explore, Imagine and Entertain' have been integrated into other units rather than given units of their own because experience has shown that these two elements are taught best when they arise from other work.

All activities and assignments that provide work to be entered for 'Personal and Imaginative Writing' coursework are indicated by the following icon:

All opportunities for 'Speaking and Listening' practice and assessment are indicated by:

All examples of 'Exam Practice' questions at both Foundation and Higher Tier are indicated by:

Activities and assignments requiring Writing are marked by the following icon:

Activities and assignments marked by the following icon require Thinking only:

In Units 1 and 2, where some of the more difficult words haven't been explained in the text, helpful glossary notes are provided. In Unit 1, as students will study only one of either Collection A, B or C, they are referred to the page where the definition first appears.

Students are also asked to take an active approach, by independently looking up some of the more difficult words in a dictionary.

As there are now two specifications to choose from, you need to remind yourself of the differences between them:

Specification A:

✱ Work reflecting 'Different Cultures and Traditions' is a coursework element.

✱ Non-fiction is based on the *Edexcel Anthology for GCSE English* and is tested in Papers 2F/4H.

✱ Media is unprepared and tested in Papers 3F/5H.

Note: If you are preparing students for this specification then the 'Different Cultures and Traditions' unit of this book, though based on the *Edexcel Anthology* (required for Specification B), provides suitable material, activities and assignments for coursework.

Specification B:

✱ Response to Media Texts is a coursework element.

✱ Work reflecting 'Different Cultures and Traditions' is based on the *Edexcel Anthology* and tested in Paper 2F/4H.

✱ Non-fiction is unprepared and tested in Paper 4F/5H.

Note: If you are preparing students for this specification, there is a suitable Media coursework assignment on pages 187–190. Students can be prepared for the Non-fiction examination question by following the *Edexcel Anthology*-based unit on pages 83–116.

The *Teacher's Resource* that accompanies this coursebook also contains material to support the 'Pre-1914 Poetry and Pre-1914 Prose' elements of GCSE English Literature coursework.

To the student

To make the most of this book we suggest you do the following:

✱ Try to become familiar with the assessment objectives for each element of the course.

✱ Make the most of the opportunities for 'Speaking and Listening'. As well as helping you to learn, these activities can be assessed to provide 20% of your marks.

✱ Think hard about your note-making skills. Many of the units ask you to make notes and they will be invaluable as revision aids. Make sure that they are effective.

✱ Pay special attention to language; notice the way a writer chooses and uses words. This is obviously important in the study of poetry but it will also gain you marks when responding to any of the reading on the course.

✱ Keep a dictionary to hand during lessons and homework. You will encounter new words during the course and you need to increase your vocabulary as much as you can.

✱ Many of the activities in this book require pair or small group work. Be sure that you work well and communicate effectively within your pairs or groups, so that you benefit from other people's ideas and they gain from yours.

This helpful table shows, at-a-glance, the details of the two specifications and the differences between them.

Edexcel GCSE English A (1203)	Edexcel GCSE English B (1204)
Coursework	**Coursework**
Speaking and Listening (20%)	*Speaking and Listening (20%)*
✱ 3 assessments	✱ 3 assessments
Written Coursework (20%)	*Written Coursework (20%)*
✱ Personal and Imaginative Writing (10%)	✱ Personal and Imaginative Writing (10%)
✱ Different Cultures and Traditions (5%)	✱ Media Texts (5%)
✱ Shakespeare (5%)	✱ Shakespeare (5%)
Examinations	**Examinations**
Examination One (2 hours)	*Examination One (2 hours)*
✱ Modern Poetry (Anthology)	✱ Modern Poetry (Anthology)
✱ Non-fiction Prose (Anthology)	✱ Different Cultures and Traditions (Anthology)
✱ Writing to Inform, Explain, Describe	✱ Writing to Inform, Explain, Describe
Examination Two (2 hours)	*Examination Two (2 hours)*
✱ Media Texts (Unseen)	✱ Non-fiction Prose (Unseen)
✱ Writing to Argue, Persuade, Advise	✱ Writing to Argue, Persuade, Advise
✱ Writing to Analyse, Review, Comment	✱ Writing to Analyse, Review, Comment

① Modern Poetry

UNIT

The Specifications

Response to poetry is examined in both the English specifications and the English Literature specification. The same unit of poetry may be studied for both.

English A (1203); B (1204)

THE CRAFT OF THE WRITER

Papers 2F (Foundation Tier) or 4H (Higher Tier)
Section A: Modern Poetry

There will be **one** question set on each of the three thematic collections of poetry in the *Edexcel Anthology*:
In Such a Time as This; Identity; Nature.
You must answer **one** question, which will be assessed for reading, based on close reading of **one** of the prepared themes, showing sustained interpretation of content, language and presentation. The questions will focus on **at least two** poems. Questions may focus on two or three named poems, or on a named poem and a poem or poems chosen by the student from the collection. This means that all the poems must be studied in the chosen thematic collection.

Assessment Objectives

You are required to demonstrate the ability to read with insight and engagement, making appropriate references to texts and developing and sustaining interpretations of them. You are further required to understand and evaluate how writers use linguistic, structural and presentational devices to achieve their effects; and to comment on the ways language varies and changes.

English Literature (1213)

Papers 2F (Foundation Tier) and 3H (Higher Tier)
Section A: Modern Poetry

There will be **two** questions set on each of the three thematic collections of poetry in the *Edexcel Anthology*:
In Such a Time as This; Identity; Nature.

You must write about a minimum of **two** poems, **at least one** of which will be named in the question. You will be required to compare that poem with at least one other poem, which may be named, or may be selected by you.

Note that the two examinations, in English and English Literature, will refer to different named poems.

Assessment Objectives

You will be asked to explore relationships and comparisons between poems, selecting and evaluating relevant material, and to explore the language, structure and form of the poems.

If you are studying for GCSEs in English and English Literature, your study of poetry will count twice. The poetry included in the *Edexcel Anthology* provides you with the opportunity to read and discuss a wide variety of poems split up into thematic collections. Your teacher will select one of the collections for you to study.

To help you get started, what follows is a general guide to working with any poem. Some of this advice will certainly be familiar to you, but it is a useful reminder of how to tackle a poem.

Tackling a Poem

Poetry isn't immediately straightforward to understand because it uses a variety of conventions and techniques that we don't use in everyday speech and writing. The trick is not to let poetry scare you, by knowing how to tackle it.

Taking the plunge ...

Firstly, fairly obviously, you should begin by **reading** the poem through, all in one go (even if you don't understand all of it). If the poem is divided into verses, a different person could read each one so that you get a feel for the structure of the poem.

Second stage: read the poem through again, more slowly, jotting down anything you find interesting or difficult to understand.

Think about the title – what does it refer to? Can you predict from the title what the poem will be about?

Consider the tone of the poem – would you say it is serious, funny, ironic, or angry, and so on?

Poetry can generally be divided into two groups:

✱ those that tell some kind of a story, or have a 'narrative' structure

✱ those where the author expresses a series of thoughts or observations.

Think about which category the poem fits into, but remember that occasionally a poem can be in both groups.

Now consider what the author is writing about. Sometimes poetry seems to be about one thing but is actually about another. A poem should have at least one theme, a sort of central concept that pulls it all together.

What is the mood of the poem? Mood is created by the expression of feelings and emotions that are aroused in the reader. Think about what the poem does to you and whether you think the author intended it to do that.

What is the poet's viewpoint: the way he or she sees the ideas and issues that have been introduced?

Third stage: once you have mastered the basics you can really begin to understand the poem, to get to know it and how it works. This stage involves more 'close reading' – you will need to look at tiny details in the poems.

Start by looking at the shape of the poem. Is there a recognisable form? Is it divided into verses and if so, why do you think that is? Do the verses follow on from one another or do they deal with different issues? You could try giving the verses sub-headings in order to see how the poem moves through its ideas.

Does the poem have a rhyme scheme? Is there a regular rhythm? It may help you to read 'Death in Leamington' (page 8 of *The Edexcel Anthology for GCSE English*), even if you are not studying it. You will notice a definite 'beat', and the fact that the second and fourth lines of each verse rhyme. Several of the poems have a less obvious rhyme or none at all. At the beginning of 'Digging' (page 21 of the *Edexcel Anthology*) the poet uses a near rhyme rather than a pure rhyme, where the first two lines end with 'thumb' and 'gun'. When the words have the same vowel sound but do not make a pure rhyme, then the poet is using assonance. If a poem does not have a rhyme or rhythm it is called free verse.

Think about how the form, style and rhythm are suited to the subject matter. The poet has deliberately chosen to represent the material in a certain way. Why do you think the poet has arranged the poem like that? Consider how it would be different if it was written in prose instead of as a poem.

Think about punctuation – remember that a line is not necessarily a sentence, so it isn't always helpful to tackle a poem line by line. One of the poems, 'Iguana Memory' (page 38 of the *Edexcel Anthology*), does not have any punctuation, and if you write about this poem this is something you should refer to. Why do you think the poet has punctuated (or not punctuated) the poem in this way?

Think about the different levels of meaning in the poems. Does the poet use puns: words that have two or more meanings? For example in 'Refugee Blues' (page 15 of the *Edexcel Anthology*), when the poet says 'Went to a committee; they offered me a chair', we might not be sure whether he was simply offered a seat or whether he was asked to be the chairperson. Think about whether the poet is being deliberately ambiguous, and if so, the reasons why. It might be to challenge the reader to work out what is really meant, or to suggest that truth is never simple.

The language of a poem is probably what most distinguishes it from ordinary writing. You will need to spend some time thinking about the words and phrases the author has chosen, always remembering to ask why the poet has used a particular word. Would another word have achieved the same effect? For this you need to be aware of some technical terms that will make your discussion and understanding of the poems easier.

The Language of Poetry

Poets think very hard about the language they use to make it 'poetic'. You should be able to identify the techniques and features they use, but in the examinations you should always remember to say not just how the poet writes, but why. Here are some of the main features for you to be aware of:

Imagery

Poets do not deal with facts and figures. They prefer instead to create pictures in the reader's mind, which at the same time will produce feelings in the reader's heart (or wherever it is we have feelings). To put it more simply, an image will appeal directly to one or more of our five senses: sight, sound, touch, taste and smell.

Some images are fairly straightforward and simply to be taken at face value. 'Warning' (page 29 of the *Edexcel Anthology*) begins, for example, with the poet imagining herself in old age wearing 'purple with a red hat which doesn't go'.

Other images use comparisons to try to take you to the heart of an experience. In the poem 'Trout' (page 45 of the *Edexcel Anthology*), for example, the poet uses a metaphor, referring to the fish as 'a fat gun-barrel' and continues the idea in words like 'torpedoed', 'fired', 'tracer-bullet' and so on, in order to capture something of its explosive power. The same poet also describes the trout's rhythmical beauty in the simile 'slips like butter down the throat of the river'. You'll have noted that a metaphor takes the comparison for granted, whilst a simile actually draws your attention to it, generally with a word such as *like* or *as*.

Alliteration

Alliteration is where the poet uses words in quick succession that start with the same letter. Notice how the heavy alliteration of the first line of 'The Thought-Fox' (page 36 of the *Edexcel Anthology*) captures the mood of a long and lonely night: 'I imagine this midnight moment's forest'.

Onomatopoeia

Onomatopoeic words are words that imitate sounds, which means that they are particularly effective because they appeal directly to our senses. Notice how in lines 8 and 9 of 'Death of a Naturalist' (page 18 of the *Edexcel Anthology*), the poet refers to the 'warm thick *slobber* of frogspawn' (our italics) and later to the 'slap and plop' of the emerging frogs.

And finally . . .

When you come to write about the poems you should be able to give a considered judgement, remembering to say not just how you feel, but being able to explain your reaction.

In the English Literature examination you will have to compare two poems of a similar theme. The following bullet points are always useful to refer to when comparing and contrasting poems:
- setting and atmosphere
- vocabulary and language
- imagery
- rhyme and rhythm
- viewpoint.

Collection A: In Such a Time as This

The poems in this collection mirror our lives. They can be divided into 'times' such as these: **Childhood Memories**; **New Beginnings**; **War and Death**; although you will notice that some could fit into more than one category.

The **Childhood Memories** poems reflect the fears and uncertainties of that time in our lives. 'Half-past Two' and 'Hide and Seek' are about very young children, whilst 'Brendon Gallacher' is *real* for the child who plays with her imaginary friend, only to suffer the grief of *death* when the reality is discovered. In 'Lucozade' a girl visits her demanding mother in hospital, whom she fears is dying, whilst 'Yellow' and 'The House' are recollections of childhood, neither very happy.

The poems about **New Beginnings** are varied: they include 'Electricity Comes to Cocoa Bottom', which tells of the excitement at seeing electric light for the first time; a poem by Thomas Hardy about the turn of the century – but the century before our own Millennium ('The Darkling Thrush'); and two poems about people who have experienced making 'new beginnings' in this country.

The poems about **War and Death** range from the Greek/Trojan attitudes to war when fighting was hand-to-hand (an extract from 'War Music'); to World War I described in the vivid poetry of Wilfred Owen; while 'Refugee Blues' by W.H. Auden is a story of rejection in World War II. Also included is 'Death in Leamington', which depicts a quiet death, so very different from the violence of death in war.

In all the poems in this collection there are many reflections on life today – and how strangely unchanging the world is.

The poet, playwright and novelist, Jackie Kay, has three poems in this section, 'Brendon Gallacher', 'Yellow' and 'Lucozade', all of which deal

sensitively with relationships. She was born in 1961, in Edinburgh. Her mother was Scottish and her father was Nigerian. She was adopted by a white couple and brought up in Glasgow. Her adopted parents were Communists who took their children on anti-apartheid protests and peace rallies.

The war poet, Wilfred Owen, was killed in action at the end of World War I. Through his poetry he gave people new insights into the reality of war: mud, mustard gas, men so exhausted they marched 'asleep'. His language was startling, vivid, memorable. He has been called the greatest war poet of all time. He believed that, 'All a poet can do is to warn,' and that, 'The poetry is in the pity.'

Childhood Memories

POEMS WITHIN *IN SUCH A TIME AS THIS* THAT DEAL WITH THE THEME OF CHILDHOOD MEMORIES

'Half-past Two' by U.A. Fanthorpe
'Hide and Seek' by Vernon Scannell
'Brendon Gallacher' by Jackie Kay
'Lucozade' by Jackie Kay
'Yellow' by Jackie Kay
'The House' by Matthew Sweeney

'Half-past Two'

BY U.A. FANTHORPE

Before Reading

Discuss in pairs, or as a class:

✱ Can you recall being 'told off' as a child? List words that describe the way you felt at the time.

✱ The poem contains the phrase 'the clockless land of ever'. What do you think it might mean?

Exploring the Poem

In pairs, discuss and make brief notes in response to the following questions.

Language and Style

1. Why do you think the poet uses such simple language?

2. Who is saying the words in brackets?

3. Why does the poet use capital letters for some words? What difference do they make to the poem?

4. How does the poet show us the child's idea of time? Do you think it is effective?

5. How does the poet let us know that it is the child telling the story?

6. When we look back to the past with delight, we are being **nostalgic**. Could this poem be described as nostalgic?

Themes

What does the poem have to say about the following themes?
- ▶ the boy's home
- ▶ the boy's imagination
- ▶ the nature of childhood.

Links with other Poems

This poem links to 'Hide and Seek', as they both describe the experiences of young children.

WRITING BASED ON THE POEM

Write a child's eye view of an incident where time seems either to stand still or go very fast. You may write a narrative, poem, diary or a letter.

'Hide and Seek'

BY VERNON SCANNELL

Glossary

Nostalgia/ Nostalgic: a longing for what is past; sentimental memories of past happiness, not always entirely true.

Before Reading

Discuss in pairs, or as a class:

✱ Do you remember in childhood games such as Hide and Seek and Sardines, waiting for someone to find you? How did you feel?

✱ Were there any occasions when you lost out – when it went wrong – or when *you* defeated someone else by a trick?

Exploring the Poem

In pairs, discuss and make brief notes in response to the following questions.

Language and Style

1 Do you think the child has played this game before? What **imperatives** at the beginning of the poem show this?

2 Who is telling us how the child feels? Is he comfortable or uncomfortable? What phrases tell us?

3 What unusual word is used when the 'seekers' arrive? What does it add to the poem? See how many **verbs** you can find that show their actions.

4 What does the toolshed smell of? What does the poet's use of a simile here make you think of? Write down all the words that are held together **alliteratively** throughout the poem by the letter 's' to show this smell.

5 The poem is written in the present tense. What does it add to the story – would it be different if it were in the past tense?

6 Tell the story as you think the boy would tell it to the grown-ups when he eventually returned to the house.

7 Can this poem be described as ironic? If necessary, see the glossary note on page 20 to check its meaning.

Themes

What does the poem have to say about the following themes?
- ▶ the boy's childhood
- ▶ learning experiences in life.

Links with other Poems

This poem links with that of the girl in 'Brendon Gallacher', in that they both experience a painful moment of growing up. It also links with 'Half-past Two' as it is the memory of a very small child who finds himself alone.

Glossary

Imperative: a form of the verb used to express commands.

Verb: a word in a sentence that enables us to say what people or things are doing.

Alliteration: the repetition of initial letters in order to gain a special effect, e.g. the forest's ferny floor.

WRITING BASED ON THE POEM

Write the story from the point of view of one of the 'seekers': what he or she did, what he or she thought and why he or she tricked the other child. Imagine what happened when the boy eventually returned to the house.

'Brendon Gallacher'

BY JACKIE KAY

Before Reading

Discuss in pairs, or as a class:

* Have you ever had an imaginary friend? If so, what was he or she like?

* Why do you think children often have imaginary friends?

Exploring the Poem

In pairs, discuss and make brief notes in response to the following questions.

Language and Style

1 Does the poem rhyme, and what difference does this make?

2 How many verses are there, and how many lines in each verse?

3 How many facts can you discover about Brendon in the poem?

4 List the differences between Brendon's 'family' and the child's family. How does the poet differentiate between the two?

5 Note the repetition of 'my' throughout the poem. What effect does this have?

6 Where did the child always 'meet' Brendon? Why was she indoors on the day 'he died'?

7 Discuss the repetition of 'one day'. Why is it repeated and what does it lead up to?

Themes

What does the poem have to say about the following themes?
▶ the child's imagination
▶ the child's home life
▶ loneliness.

Links with other Poems

In 'Brendon Gallacher' we are given a very clear picture of a *person* who *died*, which can be compared with the description of the old lady who died in 'Death in Leamington', but whom we only learn about from her lifestyle and surroundings.

In 'Lucozade' we explore the relationship of the girl to her mother as in 'Brendon Gallacher', the poet describes her relationship with her imaginary friend.

WRITING BASED ON THE POEM

Write a story about a lonely child and his or her imaginary friend. Bring it to a surprising or unexpected end.

'Lucozade'

BY JACKIE KAY

Before Reading

Discuss in pairs, or as a class:

✳ Have you ever visited anyone in hospital?

✳ Did you take a present? If you were in hospital what would you like to be given?

Exploring the Poem

In pairs, discuss and make brief notes in response to the following questions.

Language and Style

1. Is the opening of the poem optimistic or pessimistic? What about the last line of the poem – does it have a different **tone**, or not?

2. Which lines rhyme? Look for the mid-rhymes in the poem: what difference do they make to the *sound* of the poem?

3. How does the poet emphasise how demanding the mother is?

4. What picture have you built up of a) the mother; b) the daughter? List the words and phrases the poet uses that make you think this.

5. The mother finds the 'empty table is divine' when her daughter leaves with her 'bags full'; how does the poet describe the effect on the mother? Do you think this is effective? Why?

Themes

What does the poem have to say about the following themes?
  ▶ the relationship between the girl and her mother
  ▶ the girl's wish to please her mother
  ▶ the mother's character.

Links with other Poems

This poem links with 'Brendon Gallacher', as they are both poems about a particular relationship.

Glossary

Tone: the poet's overall attitude to the subject matter, which might, for example, be humorous or serious.

WRITING BASED ON THE POEM

Structure a situation between two people, where you show what one of them *says* and what the other *does or thinks*, to explore the relationship between them. Choose either a narrative, playscript or poem format.

'Yellow'

BY JACKIE KAY

Before Reading

Discuss in pairs, or as a class:

✱ What does the title 'Yellow' suggest the poem is about? Brainstorm as many thoughts and ideas as the colour suggests to you.

Exploring the Poem

In pairs, discuss and make brief notes in response to the following questions.

Language and Style

1 Look carefully at the layout. It looks like prose. What makes it a poem?

2 From whose **viewpoint** do we see the poem? Do you think this is effective?

3 What impression do we gain of the girl's mother? How does the poet give us this impression?

4 How many instances of **personification**, **metaphor** and **simile** can you find? Describe what you think they add to your understanding of the poem.

5 What do you think 'passionate beetroot balls' means?

6 How many instances of bird imagery can you find? Why do you think the poet uses these?

7 What does the word 'chirping' add to the reader's image of her brother?

8 Do you think this poem is about the colour yellow – or about the poet's family?

9 Why do you think the poet called her poem 'Yellow'?

Themes

What does the poem tell us about the following themes?
  ▶ the poet's relationship with the other members of her family
  ▶ their interaction with each other
  ▶ the way in which a colour can *colour* important moments in life.

Glossary

Viewpoint: the point of view from which something is seen.

Personification: a special kind of metaphor in which an object or idea is described as though it were a person.

Metaphor: a way of comparing two or more things without using the words 'like' or 'as'.

Simile: a way of comparing things in an unusual way, using 'like' or 'as'.

Links with other Poems

The childhood memories in 'Yellow' link it with: 'Hide and Seek', 'Lucozade', 'Half-past Two', 'Brendon Gallacher' and 'The House'.

WRITING BASED ON THE POEM

Write a poem about a colour that means a lot to you. Try to bring out its associations and the feelings it gives you. Write in **free verse** without rhyme, so that your meaning is uppermost.

'The House'

BY MATTHEW SWEENEY

Before Reading

Discuss in pairs, or as a class:

✱ Describe your own house or flat in as much detail as you can. When you have finished, keep it to compare with Matthew Sweeney's poem.

Exploring the Poem

In pairs, discuss and make brief notes in response to the following questions.

Language and Style

1 Describe the structure of the poem. Does it rhyme, or is it in **free verse**?

2 How does the poet describe the bedrooms? List the verbs he uses and decide if you think it would be a pleasant place to live.

3 What word is used to describe the rat's activities? Is it an effective word to use?

4 How does the poet show how frightening a child would find the dead bodies in the house?

5 Why is the word 'hosted' a strange word to use in this situation? When is the word 'hosted' most commonly used?

6 How does the poet tell us that life outside the house is also unpleasant?

7 What wildlife is there? Find some examples of alliteration from line 20 onwards and say what they add to the poem.

Glossary

Free verse: poetry that can sometimes be regarded as *poetic prose*. It has rhythm but no definite sense of rhyme.

8 What other animals (not wild) live there – and why does the poet find that even they leave unhappy memories?

9 Look carefully at the last two lines of the poem. What word tells us that these lines will be different in tone to the rest of the poem?

10 Why should a 'piano' leave pleasant memories? Why does the boy think the fact that he 'grew up there' made the house a better place?

Themes

What does the poem have to say about the following themes?
▶ the boy's feelings about his childhood home
▶ the boy's family life
▶ the effect of surroundings upon people.

Links with other Poems

This poem links with the other poems in the **Childhood Memories** section, although while the poet's recollection of his entire childhood is particularly unhappy, the other *childhood memories* contain only moments of unhappiness.

 **WRITING BASED ON THE POEM**

Write a descriptive passage, with carefully chosen metaphors, similes and **adjectives**, entitled *The Strange House*. (Do *not* turn it into a story, but write it so that it could be *used* in a story.)

Glossary

Adjective: a word which helps to give more information about a noun or pronoun (describing word).

New Beginnings

'Wherever I Hang'

BY GRACE NICHOLS

Before Reading

Discuss in pairs, or as a class:

✱ What sort of problems might face someone who moves to a new country? Make a list of the most important ones.

Exploring the Poem

In pairs, discuss and make brief notes in response to the following questions.

Language and Style

1 Look at the structure of the poem and describe it to each other. Who is telling the 'story'?

2 What is the meaning of the last three lines of the poem? What do they tell us about the problems the poet has encountered whilst living in two different countries and how she attempts to deal with the situation?

3 What does the last line tell us about her attitude to life generally?

4 How would you describe the language in which the poem is written? What do you think it adds to the poem?

5 Find two uses of contrast in the poem. What do they tell us of how the poet feels about the two countries to which she belongs?

6 Describe the simile in lines 12 and 13. Put it into ordinary language. What does the simile add to the poem that makes the description of life in a city more vivid?

Themes

What does the poem have to say about the following themes?

▶ the problems of knowing where one *belongs*, if one moves to a new country

▶ the importance of a person's attitude when approaching anything new.

Links with other Poems

This poem shares the theme of *roots* with 'Where the Scattering Began', but is written in a much simpler fashion.

WRITING BASED ON THE POEM

Write a short story about the (perhaps humorous?) experiences of someone coming to England for the first time, from a very different culture.

'Where the Scattering Began'

BY MERLE COLLINS

Before Reading

Discuss in pairs, or as a class:

✴ Have you always lived close to where to you live now?

✴ If not, do you miss the places and people where you lived before?

✴ How would you describe a person's *roots*? Do you think it is where a person was born, or is it something to do with ancestry?

Exploring the Poem

In pairs, discuss and make brief notes in response to the following questions.

Language and Style

1 Discuss the way this poem is written: analyse the **verse structure** and the **rhyme scheme**.

2 How does the **internal rhyme** (e.g. faces – paces) affect the rhythm?

3 List all the references to music that you can find.

Glossary

Verse structure: a pattern of lines in regular form, e.g. a sonnet has a 14-line verse structure.

Rhyme scheme: the regular pattern of rhymes in a poem.

Internal rhyme: rhymes which occur mid-line in a poem.

4 How does music influence the people in the poem?

5 How many words can you find that are linked to language (e.g. 'calls')? What is the poet saying about their *own* language?

6 What does the poet say they have added to the language they now use?

7 How many times are the words 'we come' repeated? What is the effect and importance of this? What does it lead up to?

8 This is a complex poem. Can you sum up what it is about?

Note: a *mbira* is a musical instrument played with the thumbs. It is sometimes called a *thumb piano*.

Themes

What does the poem have to say about the following themes?
  ▶ the way in which people and cultures change
  ▶ the nature of music
  ▶ the nature of *roots*.

Links with other Poems

This poem can be linked with 'Wherever I Hang', which also explores the theme of belonging. In 'Where the Scattering Began', the poem deals with a group and is generalised, while 'Wherever I Hang' focuses on an individual experience.

WRITING BASED ON THE POEM

Music is very powerful and stirs hidden emotions. Write in any way you like about an occasion when this happens or has happened. Your response may be factual or fictional.

'The Darkling Thrush'

BY THOMAS HARDY

Before Reading

Discuss in pairs:

✱ Can you remember the night of the Millennium? Were you excited at the thought of entering a new century? Share your memories with a partner.

Exploring the Poem

In pairs, discuss and make brief notes in response to the following questions.

Language and Style

1 Count the number of lines in each verse and work out how the rhyme scheme works. Would you describe 'The Darkling Thrush' as a carefully structured poem?

2 What time of day is it, on which day of which year?

3 Can you find an example of: personification, metaphor, alliteration and simile? Write them down and describe to each other what you think they mean, and what they add to the poem.

4 Find three words that we no longer use in everyday speech. What do they tell us about the poem?

5 Find three words that relate to death in lines 10 to 12. Why do you think the poet brings in these images? What else is *dying*?

6 What is the effect of the thrush's song upon the poet?

7 In the last verse the poet compares 'terrestrial things' with the 'thrush' (alliteration again!). What are the words he uses to describe the thrush that might give it *heavenly* attributes? Why do you think he does this?

Themes

What does the poem have to say about the following themes?
  ▶ the wonder of nature
  ▶ feelings of dejection.

Links with other Poems

This poem can link with 'Dulce et Decorum Est', in which the atmosphere and scene are also memorably described. However, it is a poem of **New Beginnings** and Hardy's hope for the new century, **symbolised** by the powerful song of the thrush, and so can be compared with 'Refugee Blues' in which the outlook is not so hopeful.

Glossary

Symbolise/ Symbolic: something which stands for an idea which is universal, e.g. 'the *river* of life'.

WRITING BASED ON THE POEM

Think of a time when you were feeling lonely or unhappy and something or someone unexpectedly cheered you up. Write a vivid account of the experience, in any form you choose.

'Electricity Comes to Cocoa Bottom'

BY MARCIA DOUGLAS

Before Reading

Discuss in pairs, or as a class:

✱ Imagine what life must be like without electricity. Consider the title of the poem and imagine what it must be like to experience electricity for the first time. How might it happen? What difference would it make to people's lives?

Exploring the Poem

In pairs, discuss and make brief notes in response to the following questions.

Language and Style

1 Describe the structure of this poem. Why do you think some of the lines such as 'Closing. Closing' are so short? What is the effect of this particular line?

2 The poem starts with 'Then' as if it is a continuation. What effect does this have?

3 If we think of this poem as a story, from whose viewpoint(s) do we see it?

4 Look carefully at the poem and decide who forms the *audience* for this exciting moment.

5 How do the 'fireflies', 'kling-klings', the 'breeze' and the 'bamboo' each prepare themselves for the moment? List their actions.

6 Why are the 'fireflies' described as having 'lanterns'? What is **ironic** about this?

Themes

▶ the preparation and excitement before any special occasion
▶ the moment when a new technology arrives, changing people's lives forever.

Links with other Poems

This is a poem in which night is coming, as in 'The Darkling Thrush'. It also links with 'Wherever I Hang', and the other poems in the **New Beginnings** section.

Glossary

Irony/Ironic: In speech, saying the opposite of what you mean, usually in a sarcastic tone, in order to drive your point home. In drama, a comment made by a character which turns out to have more truth than he or she realised when it was said.

WRITING BASED ON THE POEM

Write a **dialogue** about a time when you were looking forward to something that you had never experienced before. You could be going to your first football match, going on holiday to somewhere new or going on a school outing. Your dialogue could be asking someone about what to expect, or you could be discussing your expectations with a friend who has entirely different expectations. When you have finished, act it out with a partner.

'You Will Be Hearing From Us Shortly'

BY U.A. FANTHORPE

Before Reading

In pairs:

✳ Role-play a job interview. Try to make the interviewer as rude as possible without being openly insulting. The applicant really wants the job. How does he or she deal with the situation?

Exploring the Poem

In pairs, discuss and make brief notes in response to the following questions.

Language and Style

1 What is the form of this poem? Do you think it looks like a poem – or more like a series of questions?

2 Although the interviewee does not speak, how do we become aware of his or her feelings?

3 How many questions do the interviewers ask? How would you describe the tone of these questions?

4 Is the language poetic or factual? Do you think it *sounds* like an interview?

5 Write down a list of the subjects included in verses 3, 4 and 5. Do you think they are questions that *should* be asked at a job interview? If not, why not?

Glossary

Dialogue: characters' spoken words in a story or play.

6 What does the very last question imply?

7 Do you feel sympathy for the person being interviewed?

8 Read the definition of the word **satirical** in the glossary below. Do you think it describes the *tone* of this poem?

Themes

What does the poem have to say about the following themes?
- ▶ the relationship between an employer and his or her employees
- ▶ the way in which people should behave to each other.

Links to other Poems

In 'Refugee Blues', the refugees are also interviewed and rejected. In 'Hide and Seek', 'The House' and 'The Send-off', there are also victims of various sorts of abuse. In 'Death in Leamington', the person about whom the poem is written is also silent.

Glossary

Satire/Satirical: writing in which people's vices or follies are ridiculed.

WRITING BASED ON THE POEM

Write a humorous playscript of a really bizarre or peculiar interview, perhaps for an 'odd' job, such as walking the Queen's corgis or being a human cannonball in a circus.

War and Death

POEMS WITHIN *IN SUCH A TIME AS THIS* THAT DEAL WITH THE THEME OF WAR AND DEATH

'Refugee Blues' by W.H. Auden
'War Music' by Christopher Logue
'The Send-off' by Wilfred Owen
'Dulce et Decorum Est' by Wilfred Owen
'Death in Leamington' by John Betjeman

'Refugee Blues'

BY W.H. AUDEN

Before Reading

Discuss in pairs, or as a class:

✻ Refugees (now often called 'asylum seekers') move to another country because their own country is at war or they are being persecuted. Brainstorm as many ideas as you can that you associate with the word 'refugee'.

✻ This poem was written about the persecution of German Jews during World War II. What do you know of their experiences?

Exploring the Poem

In pairs, discuss and make brief notes in response to the following questions.

Language and Style

1 Analyse the structure of the poem. How many verses are there and how many lines are there to each verse? Who do you think is telling the *story*? To whom?

2 How would you describe the language: factual/poetic/emotive?

3 What repeated phrase makes this poem sound like a conversation?

4 How many comparisons can you find? What is the effect of them?

5 List the reactions of a) the consul; b) the committee; c) the speaker at a public meeting. How would you describe their attitudes to the refugees?

6 How do the refugees react? What is their attitude?

Themes

What does the poem have to say about the following themes?
- ▶ the nature of rejection
- ▶ the nature of compassion and kindness.

Links with other Poems

This poem links with 'You Will Be Hearing From Us Shortly' as they are both poems about rejection. However, it also contrasts with 'Wherever I Hang', which describes how a person new to a country starts to *belong*.

WRITING BASED ON THE POEM

Imagine that you and your family have fled from persecution in your own country and arrive in another, seeking refuge and a new life. To some people, however, you are not very welcome. Write approximately three to four diary entries, or a letter to relatives in your original country, describing some of your experiences.

'War Music'

BY CHRISTOPHER LOGUE

Before Reading

Discuss in pairs:

✱ How different is a war in the twenty-first century to the type of war between the ancient Greeks and Trojans? With a partner, make a list of the types of weapons used then and now.

Exploring the Poem

In pairs, discuss and make brief notes in response to the following questions.

Language and Style

1 Notice how the extract begins like a screenplay. What effect does this have?

2 This is an extract from a long narrative poem. How does this affect your reading?

3 What do you make of the use of the word 'jived' in line 19? Can you find any other examples of surprising or unusual choices of words?

4 Find all the words held together alliteratively by the letter 't'. What is the effect of this alliteration?

5 Put the simile describing Ajax's head into *ordinary* language. What does it tell you about his condition?

6 List the verbs describing Hector's part in the battle. Do you think they give an effective picture of his agility?

7 What did Hector intend to do? Did he succeed?

8 Now list the words used to describe Ajax. How would you sum him up?

9 What do the words 'maybe' (line 11), 'yet' (line 12), and 'But' (line 25), all lead to?

10 What did Ajax realise that made him finally give up?

11 This poem has a quite humorous tone considering its violent content. How do you feel about the use of humour?

Themes

What does the poem have to say about the following themes?
- ▶ the power of the brain over physical strength
- ▶ the nature of heroism
- ▶ the use of humour to describe violence.

Links with other Poems

This poem contrasts with 'Dulce et Decorum Est', which describes a very different war. In 'War Music' we know the individuals concerned – and the battle is *heroic*, while in 'Dulce et Decorum Est' the *battle* is horrific and the people depersonalised – a group of war-battered soldiers.

WRITING BASED ON THE POEM

Write a story in which a large and strong animal or person is defeated by a smaller and cleverer opponent. Aim to make it descriptive and humorous.

'The Send-off'

BY WILFRED OWEN

Before Reading

Discuss in pairs:

✱ Imagine a scene in which soldiers are being sent off to war. Write a brief description of the scene as you imagine it.

Exploring the Poem

In pairs, discuss and make brief notes in response to the following questions.

Language and Style

1. Now you have read the poem, was it as you expected? If not, what surprised you?

2. Look carefully at the rhyme scheme. What is unusual about it?

3. Look at the words held together alliteratively by the letter 's' in lines 1, 2 and 11. What do these words tells us?

4. Why are the soldiers garlanded with flowers? What might they be a portent of? (Look up the word *portent* if you don't know it.)

5. What things are personified in verse 2? What is the effect of their actions?

6. Would the poem be different if the poet gave the soldiers names such as Bill and Tony? How does using only 'they' or 'them' affect the poem?

7. How does the poet think the soldiers should be welcomed back after the war? What does he think will actually happen?

8. List the words and phrases Wilfred Owen uses to convey his negative and realistic attitude to war.

9. Do you think the title could be described as ironic?

10. Discuss why you think the soldiers were being sent off 'secretly'.

Themes

What does the poem have to say about the following themes?
- ▶ the reality of war: how soldiers are treated
- ▶ the attitude of those in control, e.g. The War Office.

Links with other Poems

The poet has a very powerful anti-war message that links with W.H. Auden's 'Refugee Blues' in which he, too, sends a strong message. It links too with 'Dulce et Decorum Est' – Owen's horrifying description of a gas attack on a group of soldiers.

WRITING BASED ON THE POEM

Write a short story called 'The Send-off' about a group of people going on a mysterious journey to an unknown place. You may set it in the past, the present, or the future.

'Dulce et Decorum Est'

BY WILFRED OWEN

Before Reading

Discuss in pairs, or as a class:

✱ What are your thoughts about the title of this poem, which is taken from a Latin quotation: 'It is sweet and good to die for one's country'?

Exploring the Poem

In pairs, discuss and make brief notes in response to the following questions.

Language and Style

1 Describe the rhyme scheme and verse structure of the poem. What is interesting about them?

2 Find two similes in which Owen describes the soldiers. Are they comparisons which you would expect to use when describing young soldiers?

3 How do we know that the men are exhausted?

4 How do we know that the men are in pain, even before the gas attack?

5 What is meant by 'an ecstasy of fumbling'? What are they 'fumbling' to do?

6 What does Owen mean by saying the man was 'floundering like a man in fire or lime'?

7 How do we know that Owen watched this happen? What was he watching through? What effect did it have on him? How does the poet differentiate this moment from the rest of the poem?

8 Whom does the poet wish could have seen the man's torment? What effect does he think this might have had?

9 Do you think Owen's poem gives an effective description of the reality of war? Do you think the words *compassionate* or *ironic* (or both) describe the tone of this poem?

Themes

What does the poem have to say about the following themes?
- the effect of war upon the individual soldier
- the attitude of people back home.

Links to other Poems

This poem's strong sense of atmosphere links it with Owen's poem 'The Send-off'. It also contrasts with 'War Music', a battle in which the soldiers took a more personal approach.

WRITING BASED ON THE POEM

Write a diary or a letter to a friend at home describing what has taken place. Try to express the horror of the place and what happened, and how it affected you.

'Death in Leamington'

BY JOHN BETJEMAN

Before Reading

Discuss in pairs:

* The poem begins 'She died in the upstairs bedroom'. How might it continue? Use the title to help you.

Note: Leamington Spa is a small town that gained a reputation for gentility. It might be seen to represent what is now often called *middle England*.

Exploring the Poem

In pairs, discuss and make brief notes in response to the following questions.

Language and Style

1 Look carefully at the poem. Comment on the rhyme scheme and the rhythm.

2 The poet calls both the elderly woman and the nurse 'she'. Why does he do this and what effect does it have? Would it have made a difference if he had used their names?

3 The poet uses alliteration to hold words together. Find two examples in verses 1 and 2 and say what their effect is.

4 How does the poet describe the nurse's 'soul' and 'voice'? Do you think he admires her or not? Give reasons for your answer.

5 What do you think the poet means by 'Chintzy, chintzy cheeriness'? Is this ironic?

6 What effect does the repetition of 'Do you' have? What is the material state of the house? How would you describe it?

7 What are the nurse's actions when she realises the old lady is dead? Do you think she is upset?

8 Do you think there is a difference between the way things appeared to be, e.g. the old lady being cared for in pleasant surroundings, and what was actually happening?

Themes

What does the poem have to say about the following themes?
  ▶ the difference between appearance and reality
  ▶ the nature of relationships.

Links to other Poems

This is a very *quiet* poem, but the words have a sharpness in their implication. The patient contrasts vividly with the 'difficult' mother in 'Lucozade'.

WRITING BASED ON THE POEM

Write the Nurse's logbook or diary of the events covered in the poem including the moment when she returns to collect the tea things and realises that the old lady is dead. (Does she blame herself for not realising earlier? Does she call the doctor, or tell the family?)

Collection B: Identity

Our identity is our deepest sense of ourselves: it includes our body, mind, personality, family, race, culture and religion. It is what makes each one of us the unique person we are. The poems in this collection deal with different aspects of identity: how our minds, bodies and relationships change as we grow to **Old Age**; how we have **Moments of Decision or Realisation**, and how these affect us; the nature of our **Individual Experience**, and how it unites us to, or divides us from, others.

Seamus Heaney, the Irish poet born in Northern Ireland in 1939, is the best-known poet in this collection. He has written 5 of the 16 poems discussed here. He has a strong sense of landscape, writing about it in frank and bold detail. He also sees people and their relationships, problems and deaths as part of *nature*. He has won many prizes for poetry, and the highest of all, the Nobel Prize for Literature, in 1995. He has also written many essays and plays.

Before Reading

Discuss in pairs, or as a class:

1 How important are these factors in making you the person you are, or giving you a sense of your own identity?

Appearance	**Family**
Personality	**Religion**
Abilities	**Nationality**
Ambitions	**Environment (where you live)**

Now put them in order of importance, numbering the factors from 1 to 8, with 1 being the most important. Add any other headings you think should be included as well.

2 Read the following brief self-descriptions:

a) My name is Kamaljit. I am fifteen, tallish with dark hair and eyes. I have a lively personality and am always laughing, singing or playing practical jokes on my two younger sisters. I have two wardrobes – one British, which includes my school uniform, tops, jeans and trainers – and my Pakistani wardrobe, of saris, sandals and jewellery. I am proud of my roots but intend to qualify as a doctor and stay in Britain. I hope to marry within my community and have two or three children!

b) My name's Josh. My Mum and Dad are separated but quite friendly, which means I get two lots of presents, pocket money and outings, which is great. I love football, reggae and computer games. I expect to get quite good GCSEs and want to work with computers, probably on the engineering side, not in an office. I want to get married and have kids when I am about 30, or before that if I win the lottery! I can be a bit moody but usually I'm cheerful. When I'm old I want to look back and feel that I've had a good life.

3 Now write your own *identity picture*. Try to include some of your hopes and fears as well as facts about yourself.

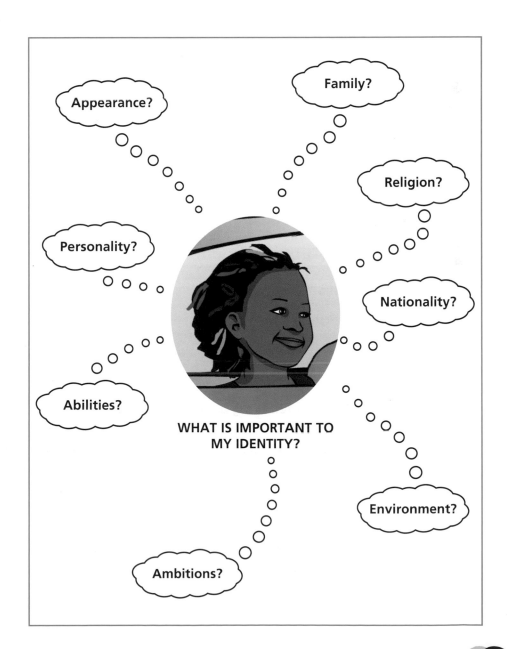

Old Age

> **POEMS WITHIN *IDENTITY* THAT DEAL WITH THE THEME OF OLD AGE**
>
> 'Warning' by Jenny Joseph
> 'Mirror' by Sylvia Plath
> 'Old Man, Old Man' by U.A. Fanthorpe
> 'Follower' by Seamus Heaney
> 'At Grass' by Philip Larkin

'Warning'

BY JENNY JOSEPH

Before Reading

Discuss in pairs, or as a class:

* How do we view youth and old age? Jot down as many words and phrases as you can that you associate with youth and old age.

Exploring the Poem

In pairs, discuss and make brief notes in response to the following questions.

Language and Style

1 How would you describe this poem: is it modern, using everyday language, or is it descriptive and poetical?

2 The first verse is eleven lines long, but the last eleven lines are divided up into three verses of four, four and three lines. Why do you think the poet does this?

3 What does the poet look forward to in old age?

4 Do you think the poem is humorous? Give examples of this.

5 What effect does the repetition of 'I shall' have?

6 How many times does the poet use 'and'? What effect does this have?

7 Do you think that this is a negative or positive poem about old age?

8 Does the poem fit in with your pre-conceptions of old age? If not, what surprised you?

Themes

What does the poem have to say about the following themes?
- ▶ the delights of old age
- ▶ the nature of freedom
- ▶ the nature of responsibility.

Links with other Poems

Contrast the positive tone of this poem with the negative tones of 'Old Man, Old Man' and 'Follower', and the fear and anxiety in 'Mirror'.

WRITING BASED ON THE POEM

Write a poem called 'Advance Notice' about how you intend to behave at some future time in your life (e.g. when a student, or married, or old) to avoid shocking people later.

'Mirror'

BY SYLVIA PLATH

Before Reading

Discuss in pairs:

✳ Can you imagine a world without mirrors? How did people manage without them?

✳ How far is your sense of your own identity based on physical appearance? Is there a *you* that is not just physical? If so, how would you explain this *self* to someone else?

✳ Is beauty only *skin deep*? Is there such a thing as *A Beautiful Mind*?

✳ How much should appearance matter?

✳ How much can you remember of a story containing the words: 'Mirror, mirror on the wall, who is the fairest of all?'

Exploring the Poem

In pairs, discuss and make brief notes in response to the following questions.

Language and Style

1 Can you find an internal rhyme? What effect does this have on the way you say the words? (See the glossary note for **internal rhyme** on page 17.)

2 Would you describe the language of this poem as factual or descriptive? Find examples to support your choice.

3 From whose viewpoint is this poem seen? How do you know this? (See the glossary note for **viewpoint** on page 13.)

4 Can you find two examples of a metaphor? Discuss with each other what they add to the meaning of the poem. (See the glossary note for **metaphor** on page 13.)

5 Why do you think that the woman would prefer to see herself by the light of the moon or candles? How does the poet emphasise this?

6 Which words tell us that the woman fears old age?

7 What impression is conveyed by the last three words of the poem?

Themes

What does the poem have to say about the following themes?
▶ the importance of physical appearance
▶ fear of old age.

Links with other Poems

This contrasts with the peaceful old age of 'At Grass', the humorous old age of 'Warning'; and compares with the changing relationships in 'Old Man, Old Man', 'Follower' and 'Once Upon a Time'.

Glossary

Monologue: a long speech spoken by one person or character.

WRITING BASED ON THE POEM

Write a **monologue** for the woman to perform as she sits in front of the mirror one morning. Begin with the phrase: 'I was young and beautiful when I first sat here …'

'Old Man, Old Man'

BY U.A. FANTHORPE

Before Reading

Discuss in pairs, or as a class:

✳ Think of any old person you know (perhaps a neighbour or relative) and write down what you know of how he or she *used to be* and how he or she *is now*. Write your points down in two columns and compare them.

✳ What do you most dread about getting old? See if you can agree on a list of six points.

Exploring the Poem

In pairs, discuss and make brief notes in response to the following questions.

Language and Style

1 Who is telling the story of this poem? Which words tell you this?

2 How can you tell when it is the old man speaking?

3 Look carefully at the poem: is there a rhyme scheme? (See the glossary note for **rhyme scheme** on page 17.) Look at the end of each verse: is there any punctuation or does it flow straight on to the next verse? Why do you think the poet does this?

4 List some examples of **slang**. How do they affect the poem?

5 Describe the character of the old man (with examples from the poem), and list his interests when he was younger.

6 Do you think he was close to his children? Find evidence to support your view.

7 Do you think his daughter feels pity for him in his old age?

8 Is she critical of him? Can you give an example?

9 Why is the last verse made up of two lines instead of three, as in all previous verses?

Themes

What does the poem have to say about the following themes?
- ▶ the girl's childhood
- ▶ changes in relationships within families
- ▶ changes in habits with different phases of life.

Glossary

Slang: a special form of language used by groups in informed situations, sometimes to add vividness or humour.

Links with other Poems

Contrasts between the past and present are also found in 'Follower', 'Once Upon a Time', and 'At Grass'. The life of this 'Old Man' may be compared to that of the old labourer in 'Miracle on St David's Day'.

WRITING BASED ON THE POEM

Imagine you are the poet's daughter. Write your diary of the day of this visit to your father, using ideas suggested both by the poem and your own imagination.

'Follower'

BY SEAMUS HEANEY

Before Reading

Discuss in pairs:

✱ Think of a time when you were a *follower*, perhaps of an older brother or sister, or a relative. Describe when and why you did this, and what the outcome was.

✱ Then listen to your partner's story.

Exploring the Poem

In pairs, discuss and make brief notes in response to the following questions.

Language and Style

1 Look carefully at the poem and discuss the verse structure. (See the glossary note for **verse structure** on page 17.) Find the rhyme scheme and count the number of syllables in each line. Are they fairly regular? If so, why do you think the poet has chosen this form for his poem?

2 Who do the first three verses describe?

3 Why did the father 'click' his tongue at the horses? How can you describe words such as 'click'?

4 Why do you think the poet uses **enjambment** at the end of verse 2 and beginning of verse 3?

Glossary

Enjambment: where the meaning and sentence flow on from line to line, or verse to verse.

5 Look at the words the poet uses and the action they describe. Do you think the *movement* of the poem reflects this action?

6 Who is described in verse 4 and 5?

7 What are the child's feelings about his father? Which words tell you this?

8 What is the change in relationships that takes place in the last verse?

9 List the many verbs used throughout this active poem to describe: a) the father; b) the adults; c) the child. What effect do they have on the poem? (See the glossary note for **verb** on page 9.)

Themes

What does the poem have to say about the following themes?
  ▶ the boy's childhood
  ▶ changing relationships with the passing of time.

Links with other Poems

'Follower' links particularly with 'Old Man, Old Man' and 'At Grass', but also has much in common with 'Once Upon a Time' – as all include vivid contrasts between past and present.

WRITING BASED ON THE POEM

One evening the adult son decides to suggest that, for his own safety, it is time that the old man went into an old people's home. The old father has always lived on the farm and loves it. Write their conversation as a playscript and bring it to a conclusion.

'At Grass'

BY PHILIP LARKIN

Before Reading

Discuss in pairs:

✱ What does the expression *put out to grass* mean?

✱ Why do you think some people look forward to retirement and others hate the thought of it?

✱ Role-play, in pairs, a dialogue between two people aged 59 and a half, with opposite feelings about their forthcoming retirements. Each person should explain their feelings to the other, and what they intend to do. (See the glossary note for **dialogue** on page 21.)

Exploring the Poem

In pairs, discuss and make brief notes in response to the following questions.

Language and Style

1 Look at the poem carefully. How many verses are there, with how many lines in each verse? What is the rhyme scheme?

2 What is the poet describing in verse 1? Can you picture the scene? Which words help you to do this?

3 Are verses 2 and 3 about the past or the present? What particular events is the poet describing? List the words that help to give a **visual image**.

4 In verses 4 and 5 how does the poet describe the contrasts between the horses' active lives and their lives in retirement? List the differences in their past and present lives.

5 Look up the words: 'artificed', 'inlay', 'almanacked', and say what these words add to the poem.

6 Pick out any words or phrases (starting with line 10) that seem associated with race courses.

Themes

What does the poem have to say about the following themes?
- ▶ the retirement of racehorses
- ▶ the peace of old age
- ▶ the nature of memories.

Links with other Poems

Its positive, happy tone links it to 'Warning', 'I Shall Paint my Nails Red', and 'Still I Rise'. Understandably, the old age of humans is seen as more problematic than that of horses.

Glossary

Visual image: words that enable the reader to 'see' what is being described in his mind's eye.

Memoirs: a person's written reminiscences of their life.

WRITING BASED ON THE POEM

One of the horses falls asleep under the tree and dreams of his past life as a race horse. Write his dream, in any way you think suitable.

Or, imagine you were the trainer of one of the retired horses and now you are retired yourself and writing your **memoirs**. Write a lively account of the horse's career and your part in it.

Moments of Decision or Realisation

> **POEMS WITHIN *IDENTITY* THAT DEAL WITH THE THEME OF MOMENTS OF DECISION OR REALISATION**
>
> 'I Shall Paint my Nails Red' by Carole Satyamurti
> 'Once Upon a Time' by Gabriel Okara
> 'Death of a Naturalist' by Seamus Heaney
> 'The Road Not Taken' by Robert Frost
> 'Mid-Term Break' by Seamus Heaney

'I Shall Paint my Nails Red'

BY CAROLE SATYAMURTI

Before Reading

Discuss in pairs, or as a class:

✱ Look carefully at the title of this poem. What is it likely to be about? Does painting your nails red sound very rebellious? Or does it depend on who is doing it?

Exploring the Poem

In pairs, discuss and make brief notes in response to the following questions.

Language and Style

1 How would you describe the structure of this poem?

2 Could it be considered a humorous poem?

3 Together, list the statements in *your* order of importance. Look up 'moratorium' to make sure you understand its meaning. Will you leave out any of the sentences?

4 What do you think the poem says about the character of the poet? Would you describe her as shy or self-assertive?

5 What is the significance of the last line?

6 Do you think this is a positive or negative approach to life? Give your reasons.

Themes

What does the poem have to say about the following themes?
  ▶ gender
  ▶ life and relationships.

Links with other Poems

The obvious one is 'Warning' by Jenny Joseph. They share an optimistic defiance of other people's expectations. Both poems are also clear statements of intention.

WRITING BASED ON THE POEM

Write a similar ten-line poem, e.g. 'I Shall Dye my Hair Green', and begin each line with a **conjunction** followed by a reason. Try to be colourful and original.

'Once Upon a Time'

BY GABRIEL OKARA

Before Reading

Discuss in pairs, or as a class:

✱ What kind of a story normally begins with the phrase 'Once upon a time . . .'?

✱ How does it usually end?

✱ What do you expect of a poem with such a title?

Exploring the Poem

In pairs, discuss and make brief notes in response to the following questions.

Glossary

Conjunction: a word used to join parts of a sentence, individual words or phrases, e.g. 'and', 'because'.

Language and Style

1 Who is the speaker in this *conversation*?

2 Who is the silent listener?

3 What does the poet mean when he says that 'Once upon a time' people would 'laugh with their hearts' not 'only laugh with their teeth'? Discuss the meaning of all *three* phrases.

4 Verses 1 to 3 tell us about experience and its effects. Write down two of the things the poet has discovered happen with experience.

5 In verses 4 to 5 he tells us what he has learned. What does he mean when he says he can 'wear many faces'?

6 Do you think the things he has learned are admirable?

7 Verses 6 to 7 are his conclusions. He wants to re-learn his innocence. What does he ask his son to teach him in the last verse?

8 What are your own feelings about the content of this poem? Can you give examples of anything you found disturbing?

9 Do you find it a negative or positive poem?

Themes

What does the poem have to say about the following themes?
  ▶ the nature of the world
  ▶ social expectations and pretence
  ▶ hope.

Links with other Poems

It links with 'Follower' and 'Old Man, Old Man', for child-parent relationships and with 'Still I Rise' for ideas about personal freedom.

WRITING BASED ON THE POEM

Write the *other side* of this conversation: the son's viewpoint, either as a playscript, poem or diary entry.

'Death of a Naturalist'

BY SEAMUS HEANEY

Before Reading

Discuss in pairs, or as a class:

✱ Can you recall any unpleasant or frightening experiences with animals or insects when you were younger?

✱ If so, what effect did the experience have on you?

Note: A flax-dam was a pool of still water used in Ireland as part of the process of making flax into linen. The flax stayed in the water for three weeks and rotted, causing an extremely unpleasant smell.

Exploring the Poem

In pairs, discuss and make brief notes in response to the following questions.

Language and Style

1 Look at the poem carefully. What is the verse structure? Does it rhyme or is it in free verse? (See the glossary note for **free verse** on page 14.)

2 Name the varieties of small wildlife that lived in the flax-dam.

3 How does the poet appeal to the sense of *sight*, *sound* and *smell*? Find one example of each.

4 Look for two examples of a simile or a metaphor: discuss with each other their meanings and what they add to the poem. (See the glossary note for **simile** on page 13.)

5 Find two examples of **onomatopoeia**, and discuss their effect on the poem.

6 The poem falls into three parts: lines 1 to 10; 11 to 21; 22 to 33. Can you see why?

Themes

What does the poem have to say about the following themes?
  ▶ the nature of fear and disgust
  ▶ the importance of childhood experiences.

Links with other Poems

Heaney's 'The Barn' and 'Mid-Term Break' are also about childhood experiences and personal growth.

Glossary

Onomatopoeia: a word or phrase whose sound gives a kind of echo of its meaning, e.g. 'crash', 'hiss'.

First person: the person speaking, e.g. 'I' or 'we'.

WRITING BASED ON THE POEM

Write about a real or imaginary encounter with some aspect of nature (an animal, insect, reptile, extreme weather conditions), which provokes a strong emotional response. Write, using the **first person**, in any form you wish.

'The Road Not Taken'

BY ROBERT FROST

Before Reading

Discuss in pairs, or as a class:

✱ Can you recall any time that you had a difficult decision to make (e.g. Year 10 options, future career, a personal matter)?

✱ How did you make the decision?

✱ Do you think now that it was the right or wrong decision? Why?

Exploring the Poem

In pairs, discuss and make brief notes in response to the following questions.

Language and Style

1 Discuss the verse form and find the rhyming pattern.

2 Do you think the poem sounds conversational and as though the poet is confiding in you? How do you think the poet does this?

3 List the facts that you learn about the woods. Although there are no obvious metaphors or similes, do you think this is a descriptive poem? Give examples of how the poet creates this effect.

4 Why does the poet take his chosen path? What was his reasoning?

5 What do you think his choice symbolises? (See the glossary note for **symbolise** on page 19.)

6 Do you think the poem sounds positive and happy? What words and phrases make you think that?

7 Do you think the poet was pleased with his choice?

Themes

What does the poem have to say about the following themes?
  ▶ making choices
  ▶ the reasons behind decisions
  ▶ living with the consequences of our choices.

Links with other Poems

This shows that the poet has a positive view of himself and his own actions, as do the poets in 'Digging', 'Still I Rise', and 'I Shall Paint my Nails Red'. Like 'Death of a Naturalist' it recounts a metaphorical as well as an actual experience.

WRITING BASED ON THE POEM

Write a short story or opening chapter of a novel in which your main character has to make a crucial decision.

For example, he or she has to decide whether:
▶ to get married
▶ to leave home.

Describe his or her thoughts and feelings.

'Mid-Term Break'

BY SEAMUS HEANEY

Before Reading

Discuss in pairs, or as a class:

✳ What do you usually do in your half-term holidays?

✳ How did you spend your last one?

✳ Write down five adjectives to describe how you normally feel when you get to half-term. (See the glossary note for **adjective** on page 15.)

Exploring the Poem

In pairs, discuss and make brief notes in response to the following questions.

Language and Style

1 In verse 1, what do we think has happened to the child?

2 Who, in fact, has died? What happened to him?

3 What was the child's reaction to the sympathy of people who came to condole?

4 From whose point of view is the poem mainly written?

5 Pick out examples of when you are given the viewpoint of other people.

6 As many of the verses are enjambed, so that the meaning flows on from verse to verse, the full stops come in unexpected places. Find one of these and say what it adds to the poem.

7 Why are lines 21 to 22 the only lines that rhyme?

Themes

What does the poem have to say about the following themes?
 ▶ the feeling of embarrassment when given sympathy
 ▶ the nature of grief
 ▶ different kinds of anger.

Links with other Poems

The element of surprise links it to 'Warning' and 'Miracle on St David's Day'. In its exploration of childhood experiences it also links together with the other Heaney poems included in the *Edexcel Anthology*.

WRITING BASED ON THE POEM

Glossary

Third person: the person spoken about.

Imagine that the poet returns to school. How might his friends treat him? Write a short piece in which you describe his feelings and experiences once he is back at school. You could write in either the first or the **third person**.

Individual Experience

POEMS WITHIN *IDENTITY* THAT DEAL WITH THE THEME OF INDIVIDUAL EXPERIENCE

'Miracle on St David's Day' by Gillian Clarke
'The Barn' by Seamus Heaney
'An Unknown Girl' by Moniza Alvi
'Not My Best Side' by U.A. Fanthorpe
'Still I Rise' by Maya Angelou
'Digging' by Seamus Heaney

'Miracle on St David's Day'

BY GILLIAN CLARKE

Before Reading

Discuss in pairs, or as a class:

✱ What do you think about miracles: are they just stories? Do they really happen? Do you believe in them? Do you know anyone who has experienced one?

Exploring the Poem

In pairs, discuss and make brief notes in response to the following questions.

Language and Style

1 How does the poet make the style of the poem conversational, appearing like a running commentary on her strange afternoon?

2 Where is she and what is she doing?

3 What do the people listening do when she reads to them?

4 Who are the last four verses mainly about?

5 Why is the poet 'afraid'?

6 As the man speaks, what happens to those listening? List their reactions.

7 All the other seven verses have five lines: why do you think there are only three lines in the last verse? Does it indicate a change of tone? (See the glossary note for **tone** on page 12.)

8 What do you think the title of the poem means and is it appropriate?

Themes

What does the poem have to say about the following themes?

▶ personal identity and loss of it
▶ the nature and importance of memory.

Links with other Poems

This poem is partly about change and therefore has positive links with 'Warning', 'I Shall Paint my Nails Red', and 'Still I Rise'. It also links with poems of more negative change such as 'Follower', 'Old Man, Old Man', and 'Mirror'.

WRITING BASED ON THE POEM

Write *either*: a short story about how the 'big, mild man' came to be 'dumb' and in the mental hospital; *or* Gillian Clarke's diary for the day she went to read 'poetry to the insane'.

'The Barn'

BY SEAMUS HEANEY

Before Reading

Discuss in pairs, or as a class:

✱ Do you remember a time when you were younger, when a place really frightened you? Write brief notes on what you can remember about it.

Exploring the Poem

In pairs, discuss and make brief notes in response to the following questions.

Language and Style

1 Look carefully at the verse form. How many syllables are there in each line? What is the pattern of the rhyme?

2 Find the two similes in the first verse. What do they mean and what do they add to the picture that is being described?

3 Verse 2 is also very **pictorial**. Can you describe the barn from it?

4 Do you think the barn was warm or cold? Which words make you think this?

Glossary

Pictorial: a visual image, as in a picture.

5 Name the animals and birds that lived in the barn. What do you think the poet was describing with the words: 'bright eyes stared . . . fierce, unblinking'?

6 Why did the poet find the barn an unpleasant place? Find two phrases that describe his feelings and fears.

Themes

What does the poem have to say about the following themes?
- ▶ the boy's childhood
- ▶ the nature of fear in childhood
- ▶ the borders of reality and nightmare.

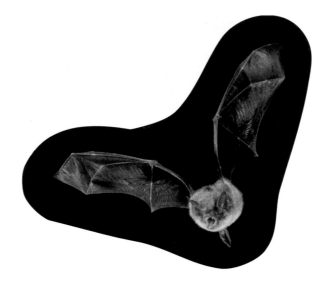

Links with other Poems

This poem shares the theme of unpleasant childhood experiences with 'Mid-Term Break', and 'Death of a Naturalist'; and semi-pleasant childhood experiences with 'Follower', all by Seamus Heaney.

WRITING BASED ON THE POEM

The boy in the poem has been having a lot of bad dreams, and has been asked to write them down when he wakes up. This is to help him and his therapist to understand them better. Imagine that you are the boy. Write down the boy's dream as shown in the last two verses of the poem, adding any other details of your own. Use the first person singular ('I').

'An Unknown Girl'

BY MONIZA ALVI

Before Reading

Discuss in pairs:

✱ Can you remember a time when a chance encounter left a vivid impression on you? Discuss it with a friend and explain why it was so important.

Exploring the Poem

In pairs, discuss and make brief notes in response to the following questions.

Language and Style

1 How would you describe the structure of this poem? Does it rhyme or is it in free verse?

2 Who is telling the *story* and what is happening to her?

3 The poem is full of colours: list as many as you can find.

4 What phrases tell you that this is not taking place in Britain?

5 Put 'She is icing my hand' into your own words.

6 The poet describes the design as 'peacock ... lines'. What does this tell us about its shape, pattern and colour?

7 Find two similes or metaphors, and discuss how they help you to understand the different culture that the poem describes.

Themes

What does the poem have to say about the following themes?
   ▶ the colour and noise of a different country
   ▶ the significance of a random encounter with another person.

Links with other Poems

As a memorable experience, it links with 'The Barn', 'Mid-Term Break' and 'Miracle on St David's Day'. As a specifically feminine experience, it links with 'I Shall Paint my Nails Red' and 'Warning'.

WRITING BASED ON THE POEM

Using the poem as a starting point, write a short story or a playscript called either *Strange Meeting* or *A Brief Encounter*.

'Not My Best Side'

BY U.A. FANTHORPE

Before Reading

Discuss in pairs, or as a class:

✶ Look at the picture on page 26 of *The Edexcel Anthology for GCSE English* but cover up the lines of the poem that appear beneath it. What might the characters (including the dragon!) be saying?

Exploring the Poem

In pairs, discuss and make brief notes in response to the following questions.

Language and Style

1 How is the poem written? Describe its verse structure.

2 Does the style of the poem suit its purpose? Explain your views.

3 Look at the verses in this poem: who is the 'speaker' in each?

4 What particular object are they describing?

5 What is the dragon interested in? Find three examples that show what is worrying him.

6 How does the girl describe the dragon? Why was she doubtful about 'the boy'?

7 Why was 'St George' proud of himself?

8 Do you think he might be a satire on modern life? (See the glossary note for **satire** on page 22 to check its meaning.)

9 Do you think the tone of this poem is humorous and ironic? Explain why or why not. (See the glossary note for **ironic** on page 20.)

Themes

What does the poem have to say about the following themes?
  ▶ image and publicity
  ▶ relationships between men and women
  ▶ the nature of ambition.

Links with other Poems

Multiple viewpoints might link this poem to 'Miracle on St David's Day' (e.g. the poet's, the man's and the nurses' viewpoints), and to 'Mid-Term Break' (the boy's, the relatives' and the parents' viewpoints).

WRITING BASED ON THE POEM

Take any well-known painting, classical or modern, which depicts animals and/or people. Try to write an imaginative monologue (with a few surprises in it!) that could be spoken by one or more of the depictions.

'Still I Rise'

BY MAYA ANGELOU

Before Reading

Discuss in pairs:

✱ Discuss with a friend what you both know about the history of slavery.

✱ When and why was it stopped?

✱ How do you think the descendants of slaves feel about it?

Exploring the Poem

In pairs, discuss and make brief notes in response to the following questions.

Language and Style

1 Look at the first seven verses (apart from verse 3), their structure (four-line verses) and rhyme. At line 29 the verse form changes. Why do you think the poet makes this change?

2 The poem is written in a series of questions; make a list of them.

3 What does the poet mean when she repeats the words 'I'll rise'?

4 At the end we learn of the poet's ancestral past. How does she feel herself to be part of that past?

5 Do you think this poem, which describes the consequences of being a descendant of slaves, makes its points effectively? Give examples which you feel demonstrate this.

6 How would you describe this poem? Do you think it is positive?

Themes

What does the poem have to say about the following themes?
- ▶ overcoming obstacles in life
- ▶ establishing your own identity
- ▶ the nature of freedom
- ▶ pride and achievement
- ▶ African-American experiences.

Links with other Poems

Other poems of self-fulfilment include 'I Shall Paint My Nails Red', 'Warning', 'Digging', and 'The Road Not Taken'.

WRITING BASED ON THE POEM

Think of a situation in history or in modern life where people are oppressed or feel themselves to be second-class citizens. Try to get *inside the skin* of such a person, and write a poem or monologue expressing their point of view.

'Digging'

BY SEAMUS HEANEY

Before Reading

Discuss in pairs, or as a class:

✱ In what respect can a pen be said to be mightier than a sword or a gun?

✱ Which do you think is harder: physical work or mental work? Or are they just as hard – but in different ways?

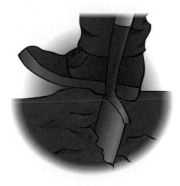

Exploring the Poem

In pairs, discuss and make brief notes in response to the following questions.

Language and Style

1 Look carefully at the poem. What is its structure? Does it rhyme or is it in free verse?

2 Are some of the lines enjambed? What effect does this have?

3 The first three verses relate to the poet's father. What was he doing?

4 Whose activities are described in lines 17 to 24? What was his expertise?

5 How does the poet plan to follow in his father's and grandfather's footsteps? What does he plan to 'dig' with?

6 What do you think he means by this?

7 This is a very descriptive poem. Pick out examples of alliteration, onomatopoeia and metaphor that you find particularly effective and explain how they *work*. (See the glossary note for **alliteration** on page 9.)

Themes

What does the poem have to say about the following themes?
  ▶ the individual in relation to his ancestral past
  ▶ carving out a role for oneself
  ▶ **literary** effort.

Links with other Poems

This poem links with other poems that involve defining oneself in relation to others, including: 'Warning', 'I Shall Paint my Nails Red', 'Miracle on St David's Day', 'Follower' and 'Still I Rise'.

Glossary

Literary: of or to do with literature. 'Literary' language tends to be poetic.

WRITING BASED ON THE POEM

Write an account of what you know about the last two to three generations of your family, including how you see yourself in relation to them. (How far are you like them? Do you want the same things?)

Collection C: Nature

The poems in this collection are about responses to the natural world, and how the writer uses nature as a source of emotion and ideas.

They are very often about animals, flowers and growing things. Natural objects are used as symbols or metaphors to express ideas about human nature. They are not concerned with man-made objects at all, except, occasionally, in the contrast these make with things of natural origin.

The poems can be divided into themes such as these: **Encounters with the Natural World**, **The Power of Nature**, and **Nature and Change**.

However, it is important to realise that other categories could have been worked out – and one poem could well find its way into another category.

The poems under the heading **Encounters with the Natural World** are about strange, fascinating moments of contact with living creatures that teach us about our own nature. Edwin Muir imagines the world after a nuclear war. 'The Horses' return to work for humans again, now that they have destroyed their own technology. Ted Hughes and a pair of 'Roe-Deer' are brought together by a snowstorm in a way that suggests humans and animals might once have lived together on more equal terms. The same poet's 'stag', however, blunders into a 'strange country' where men on horseback wait to turn dogs on him. Rosenberg, once a soldier in World War I, is startled by the sudden appearance of a superior rat that seems to mock him. In order to create poetry, Ted Hughes deliberately forces himself to imagine a fox out on its nightly prowl in 'The Thought-Fox'.

The poems under the heading **The Power of Nature** portray different aspects of the immensely powerful force of nature. Ted Hughes's 'Wind' and Theodore Roethke's 'The Storm' both capture the raging winds that make humans powerless. Seamus Heaney sees the 'Trout' as a fighting machine, always on the look out to 'pick[s] off' its prey. 'Thistles', for Hughes, never know defeat. If attacked, they come back with a vengeance. Sylvia Plath's 'Mushrooms' highlight yet another aspect, the force of nature that is gentle but cannot be resisted. It seems all these living things have a sort of natural dignity that civilised humans have lost.

The poems under the heading **Nature and Change** are linked by the theme that though nature endlessly reproduces itself, that process involves death – and for humans the sadness that we know it has to come eventually. In Thomas Hardy's 'The Five Students', the poet sees, one after another, the death of his friends who had set out in life with him, full of optimism. In 'Nettles', Vernon Scannell's young son learns an important lesson from this stinging weed that might equip him to survive in life. Grace Nichols has an 'Iguana Memory', that reminds her of the lost innocence of her childhood. Brian Patten also recognises that the older we get the more we lose contact with the natural world. We can no longer appreciate the simple beauty of 'A Blade of Grass'. In 'Flowers', Selima Hill somehow senses her daughter's response in taking flowers to her grandfather's grave is more sincere than her own. Flowers, for Jackie Kay, are also very symbolic. Adopted at birth, she remembers the pain of meeting her birth mother, in 'Keeping Orchids'. The orchids her mother gave her will wither and die because they have been cut from the stem, just as she herself was at birth.

Three of Ted Hughes's poems are present in this section. Hughes (1930–1998), a Yorkshireman, wrote lots of powerful and original poetry, most of it taking nature as its theme. For him, nature was the great creative force, but it was also something frighteningly destructive and chaotic.

In 1956, he married the American writer, Sylvia Plath, one of whose poems is also in the collection. Her suicide, in 1963, a year after their separation, stopped him writing poetry for three years. It was not for more than thirty years that he could bring himself to publish *Birthday Letters*, a tribute in verse to her. In 1984, he was made Poet Laureate.
This surprised many people who did not think his powerful style was quite right for official verses for state occasions.

Brian Patten, one of the most popular of modern British poets, was born in Liverpool's docklands, in 1946. He has remained very proud of his working-class roots.

He left school at 15 without qualifications and immediately started his own poetry magazine, appropriately called *Underdog*. Beginning in a very small way, the magazine grew in popularity and eventually had a large part to play in making poetry more widely read. Many of the so-called *Underground Liverpool* poets, those with new and radical ideas, published in it. Patten, Adrian Henri and Roger McGough were later to gain cult status among the younger generation – and also acceptance by the critics.

Many of Patten's verses have a surprising simplicity and a tender and vulnerable quality that readers find particularly appealing. One of his most popular collections was *Love Poems*, brought out in 1984, which included 'A Blade of Grass'. He is equally well known as the author of humorous children's verses, including *Gargling with Jelly* and *Thawing Frozen Frogs*.

Encounters with the Natural World

> **POEMS WITHIN *NATURE* THAT DEAL WITH THE THEME OF ENCOUNTERS WITH THE NATURAL WORLD**
>
> 'The Horses' by Edwin Muir
> 'The Thought-Fox' by Ted Hughes
> 'The Stag' by Ted Hughes
> 'Roe-Deer' by Ted Hughes
> 'Break of Day in the Trenches' by Isaac Rosenberg

'The Horses'

BY EDWIN MUIR

Before Reading

Discuss in pairs, or as a class:

✱ Imagine what life would be like after a nuclear war. How would survivors cope if modern technology was destroyed? Make a list of **adjectives** that might describe the survivors and the world they inhabit. (See the glossary note for **adjective** on page 15.)

Exploring the Poem

✱ Bearing in mind the poem was written in the mid-1950s, what might have been its background? You'll need to do some research into topics such as the Atom Bomb and the Cold War. Make notes and bring them into class to inform your work on the poem.

✱ Look at the account in *Genesis* (the first book of The Bible) of the creation of the world. The poem contains several references to the Christian account of God's creation of the world.

In pairs, discuss and make brief notes in response to the following questions.

Language and Style

1 Look at the way the poet creates a sense of mystery in the first three lines. Which adjective creates the mood most effectively?

2 'Covenant' has Biblical connotations of some kind of agreement entered into by God and his people. How appropriate and effective is the word, bearing in mind the context? Does it add to the timeless feel of the poem?

3 'Thereafter nothing': what is the effect of this two-word sentence?

4 Notice how suddenly in line 15, there comes a distinct shift in tone, mood and emphasis. Can you detect it and suggest reasons for it? (See the glossary note for **tone** on page 12.)

5 There is a **pun** on the word 'quick'. Obviously speed is suggested, but what else (in the Biblical sense of 'the quick and the dead') does it suggest? Look the word up in a dictionary and discuss its use.

6 'They waited, stubborn and shy'. Discuss the contradictions in this poem about the horses:
  ▶ they are awe-inspiring, yet beasts of burden
  ▶ they are docile yet powerful.

Themes

What does the poem have to say about the following themes?
  ▶ the old bond between humans and nature
  ▶ the nature of the relationship between humanity and technology.

Links with other Poems

The poem links to 'Roe-Deer', as they both suggest that in the past, humans and animals once enjoyed a different relationship.

WRITING BASED ON THE POEM

Write a story based on the experiences of a family on the island, surviving the nuclear war and beginning again after it. (Alternatively this could be written in the form of a diary.)

'The Thought-Fox'

BY TED HUGHES

Glossary

Pun: where a word can suggest two or more meanings at the same time.

Characteristics: are the essential qualities of something; those that form its character.

Before Reading

Discuss in pairs, or as a class:

✱ What are the **characteristics** of a fox? Find five adjectives that could be used to describe this animal.

✱ What are the characteristics of a poet? Find five adjectives that could be used to describe this type of writer.

✱ The poem is about how writing poetry can be compared to a fox going out on the prowl. Brainstorm how this might be – before checking out what Hughes is actually saying.

Exploring the Poem

In pairs, discuss and make brief notes in response to the following questions.

Language and Style

1. Comment on how the first line captures the mood of the long night where the poet is having difficulty finding inspiration. What poetic devices does the poet use to help create the effect?

2. A forest is dark and dense. Lots of dangers can be lurking in it. What does it symbolise for the poet? (See the glossary note for **symbolise** on page 19.)

3. Hughes imagines the fox moving slowly and cautiously, putting 'neat prints in the snow'. Can you spot the direct parallel here with what the writer is doing with his blank page?

4. How many words or expressions can you identify in the poem, which have a double meaning, referring both to what the fox is doing and what the writer is doing? There are at least five.

5. Why the 'sudden sharp hot stink of fox'? What point is the poet making about the moment of inspiration?

6. Which of our five senses (sight, sound, touch, taste and smell) are appealed to in the course of this poem?

Themes

What does the poem have to say about the following themes?
  ▶ the fox
  ▶ the poet's lonely struggle to create a poem.

Links with other Poems

This poem links with 'A Blade of Grass', as they are both about writing poetry.

WRITING BASED ON THE POEM

Hughes wrote elsewhere: 'In a way, I suppose, I think of poems as a sort of animal. They have their own life, like animals.' Imagine Hughes had extended this thought when writing an introduction to 'The Thought-Fox', explaining what the poem meant and how he came to write it.

'The Stag'

BY TED HUGHES

Before Reading

Discuss in pairs:

* What is your opinion of blood sports? Do you think it is cruel to hunt deer, foxes and other animals – or is it merely an effective way of keeping animal numbers at an acceptable level?

* In the poem a crowd of people has gathered to see a stag-hunt. What kind of people do you think they are likely to be? What kind of mood will they be in as they wait for it to take place?

* What is the 'bellnote of the voice that carried all the others' likely to be?

Exploring the Poem

In pairs, discuss and make brief notes in response to the following questions.

Language and Style

1. The first four verses begin with 'while' and the same word is present in the last two verses. Many lines begin with 'and'. What effect do these two words have?

2. The first four verses end with a reference to the stag. What does this achieve? Why does Hughes break the pattern in the last two verses?

3. What does he mean when he says the huntsmen 'pulled aside the camouflage of their terrible planet'? What is the poet's attitude here and what does the word 'their' tell us?

4. Discuss the ways the poet makes us have sympathy for the stag in the last two verses.

5. Consider the use of **contrast** throughout. What is achieved by it?

Themes

What does the poem have to say about the following themes?
  ▶ the nature of hunting
  ▶ the experience of being hunted.

Glossary

Contrast: occurs where two things or qualities seem to be in opposition to each other.

Links with other Poems

This poem links with 'Roe-Deer' as they both contain observations on humanity's relationship with these animals.

WRITING BASED ON THE POEM

Imagine you are one of the spectators at the hunt. Describe in detail what took place from beginning to end, and give your opinion on it. You could do it in the form of a story, a descriptive essay, a letter or a diary entry.

'Roe-Deer'

BY TED HUGHES

Before Reading

Discuss in pairs, or as a class:

✱ Can you recall being caught in a snowstorm? Do you remember how it felt at the time?

✱ When the snow falls heavily, the usual rules no longer apply. How do things change? Find examples in the poem of where people's attitudes suddenly alter.

✱ The poem refers in the first line to 'the biggest snow of the year'. Why not the 'heaviest' or the 'deepest' snow?

Exploring the Poem

In pairs, discuss and make brief notes in response to the following questions.

Language and Style

1 What effect does the poet achieve by using the unusual **compound adjective** 'dawn-dirty' – and why 'blue-dark' in preference to dark-blue?

2 What is he getting at by 'my dimension', bearing in mind he is viewing the pair of male deer through the windscreen? What other associations could the words have?

3 'Lasting seconds' has two basic meanings. What are they?

4 What is the poet getting at when he says the deer were waiting for the man to remember the 'password' and 'sign that the curtain had blown aside'?

5 The poet seems to be hinting that at one time, deer and humans met on different terms – and that briefly they have been brought together here by abnormal circumstances. What is the point about nature that is being made?

Glossary

Compound adjective: where two closely connected describing words impact on each other.

6 'The deer had come for me.' Suggest different possible meanings for this phrase.

7 After the deer had gone, the world became 'ordinary' again. What does this indicate?

8 Many of the first lines of the verses run on to the second lines, and many of the verses flow into the next. Suggest reasons for this. What effect does it have?

9 Make a list of examples of metaphorical language, and discuss the use made of it. (See the glossary note for **metaphor** on page 13.)

Themes

What does the poem have to say about the following themes?
  ▷ the effect of snow on the man
  ▷ the effect of snow on the deer
  ▷ the relationship between humans and deer now and in the past.

Links with other Poems

This poem links to 'The Stag' as they both describe humanity's relationship with this animal. It also is linked to 'The Horses' in the way it hints at a different past-relationship between humans and animals.

WRITING BASED ON THE POEM

Write about suddenly coming face-to-face with an animal, and the emotions you experience. Use as an atmospheric background an extreme form of weather, for example, a thunderstorm or a heavy fog.

'Break of Day in the Trenches'

BY ISAAC ROSENBERG

Before Reading

Discuss in pairs, or as a class:

✱ What do you imagine life was like for a British soldier on the Western Front, during World War I (1914–18), living in trenches and being constantly in fear of death?

✱ In what ways might a rat imagine itself to be far better off than one of the soldiers in the war?

Exploring the Poem

In pairs, discuss and make brief notes in response to the following questions.

Language and Style

1 Discuss how the usual roles have been reversed, with 'a queer sardonic rat' mocking the soldier and provoking the question 'what do you see in our eyes ...?' (Look up the word 'sardonic' in a dictionary, to understand its full meaning.)

2 In the summer of 1916 the poppy was not yet the symbol of the Fallen that it later became – but the popular *black* joke among the soldiers was that its very bright colour came from feeding off the blood of the dead. How does the poet use the flower as a symbol?

3 Look at the last four lines. See how the image of poppy and dust fuse together. What is being suggested?

4 What does the expression 'Bonds to the whims of murder' tell us about the poet's attitude to war?

5 Discuss the poet's use of metaphors and extended irony in this poem. (See the glossary note for **irony** on page 20.)

Themes

✳ What use does the poet make of the following symbols?
  ▶ the poppy
  ▶ the rat
  ▶ the dust
  ▶ the sleeping green.

✳ In what ways does the poet try to avoid taking sides? Why is he anxious to avoid emotional involvement with the war?

Links with other Poems

The poem links with 'The Horses', in the suggestion that animals are wiser than humankind which has the potential to destroy itself.

WRITING BASED ON THE POEM

A letter from the trenches. Use your imagination and the help of this poem to write a soldier's letter home, describing life in the middle of war, and focusing on one particular incident where a strangely knowing rat was encountered.

The Power of Nature

POEMS WITHIN *NATURE* THAT DEAL WITH THE THEME OF THE POWER OF NATURE

'Wind' by Ted Hughes
'Mushrooms' by Sylvia Plath
'The Storm' by Theodore Roethke
'Thistles' by Ted Hughes
'Trout' by Seamus Heaney

'Wind'

BY TED HUGHES

Before Reading

Discuss in pairs, or as a class:

✱ Can you ever recall being *imprisoned* in your house all day, because of bad weather outside, or because you were ill? What did it feel like?

✱ If you don't know the word *claustrophobia*, look it up in a dictionary, and discuss its meaning.

✱ When we say *we are all at sea*; what do we mean? Hughes speaks of his house having been 'far out at sea all night'. What do you imagine he has in mind?

Exploring the Poem

In pairs, discuss and make brief notes in response to the following questions.

Language and Style

1 Which words add to the dramatic opening of the poem?

2 In what ways the poet has felt threatened by the storm?

3 Find examples of the way the poet uses words that suggest noise and destruction.

4 Find the example of onomatopoeia that really brings home to us the sound of the wind blowing across the hills. (See the glossary note for **onomatopoeia** on page 42.)

5 How does Hughes personify the raging wind? (See the glossary note for **personification** on page 13.)

6 The expression 'blade-light' is so much better than a tired old **cliché** like *shafts of sunlight*. Why is it an appropriate metaphor in the circumstances?

7 Notice how beautifully the constantly changing light of the rainswept dawn is captured in the simile 'flexing like the lens of a mad eye'. Why a 'mad eye'? (See the glossary note for **simile** on page 13.)

8 Why does he use the word 'scaled' to capture his own movement?

9 What do you make of the phrase: 'tent of the hills'? Does it suggest any particular shape? What about sound? Can you imagine the drumming sound of wind on canvas?

10 Try to find other strong metaphors and similes and explain how they work.

11 In the fifth verse there is a change of tense from past to present. Can you work out why?

Themes

What does the poem have to say about the following themes?
▶ the enormous power of nature and its destructive potential
▶ humanity's emotional and physical weakness when nature gets angry.

Links with other Poems

This poem links very obviously to 'The Storm', as they both share something of the same subject matter. It also links to 'Thistles' and 'Nettles', both of which deal with Nature's power to strike at humanity.

WRITING BASED ON THE POEM

When the forces of nature become violent and do structural damage, we sometimes speak of an 'act of God'. Write about the destruction caused by high winds, or flooding, to your house, that nothing could have prevented. Imagine your feelings when trapped inside your house, waiting for things to get back to normal.

Glossary

Cliché: an expression, now used very commonly, which has lost its original freshness and appeal.

'Mushrooms'

BY SYLVIA PLATH

Before Reading

Discuss in pairs:

✳ If you had decided to write a poem about mushrooms what could you say about them? Do they have a *character*? Brainstorm ideas with a partner.

✳ If you were writing a poem of the same title, what might be its first line? Make it bright and attention-grabbing.

Exploring the Poem

In pairs, discuss and make brief notes in response to the following questions.

Language and Style

1 From whose point of view is the poem being told?

2 What contrasting qualities do the mushrooms have?

3 Notice how they are given human qualities – even though they are 'earless and eyeless'. What is being suggested here?

4 Why are they 'shelves' and 'tables'? Does the poet have more than appearance in mind?

5 Why does the repetition of 'So many of us!' occur?

6 The poem ends with an apparent self-contradiction: mushrooms are both 'nudgers and shovers' as well as being very quiet and shy by nature. What is the poet suggesting?

7 Why might 'soft fists' be said to sum up their character?

8 Do you think the poem's long and thin appearance is supposed to suggest anything? If so, what?

9 How are we reminded of Jesus Christ's teaching that 'the meek shall inherit the earth', at the end of the poem?

Themes

What does the poem have to say about the following themes?
  ▶ the force of nature
  ▶ the poet's imagination.

Links with other Poems

This poem links with 'Trout', in the way both poems show surprising characteristics of natural force and fitness.

WRITING BASED ON THE POEM

Try writing in the *voice* of a plant or vegetable. How might ivy speak, or a potato? You could write a poem or a prose monologue. (See the glossary note for **monologue** on page 34.)

'The Storm'

BY THEODORE ROETHKE

Before Reading

Discuss in pairs, or as a class:

✱ Have you seen the film *Twister*? Discuss some of its amazing special effects, and the sort of things that severe storms are capable of doing.

✱ What would the build-up to a twister be like?

✱ What precautions would you take if you knew one was on its way?

Exploring the Poem

In pairs, discuss and make brief notes in response to the following questions.

Language and Style

1 How does the first verse create the threatening atmosphere that comes before a storm?

2 How does the poet build up the tension bit-by-bit, from the sea's 'ominous lapping' to the much louder and more forceful 'swinging and slamming'?

3 Consider the poet's use of alliteration to capture the sound of the rising wind. (See the glossary note for **alliteration** on page 9.)

4 What is the effect of the large number of present participles (verbs ending in -ing)?

5 What is the effect on the tone of the poem of the rather bleak **rhetorical question**: 'Where have all the people gone?'

Glossary

Rhetorical question: a question that needs no answer, but is there for emphasis.

6 Comment on the 'steady sloshing of the swell'. What poetic device is the poet using to capture the sound and rhythm of the rising sea?

7 Comment on the effect of the sharp-sounding lines that all begin with the word 'the', and how they create for us the sudden breaking of the storm.

8 The hurricane is so strong it can 'drive the dead straw into the living pine tree'. Is this very powerful image meant to be taken literally or metaphorically – or both?

Themes

What does the poem have to say about the following themes?
- ▶ the sheer force of nature
- ▶ our sense of awe at this force
- ▶ our powerlessness against it
- ▶ how people react differently to it
- ▶ how the effects of it are felt everywhere.

Links with other Poems

This poem links to 'Wind', as they both describe the experience of being at the centre of a storm.

WRITING BASED ON THE POEM

Write a story set in Santa Lucia, California, entitled *The Twister*. Put a lot of description in it and try to show how people react to it in different ways.

'Thistles'

BY TED HUGHES

Before Reading

Discuss in pairs, or as a class:

✱ Can you describe a thistle? What are its characteristics? How would you sum it up? To help you, consider this: the thistle is the national flower of Scotland. What qualities might it have to make the Scottish people take it to their hearts?

Exploring the Poem

In pairs, discuss and make brief notes in response to the following questions.

Language and Style

1 Which word in the first verse sums up the character of the thistle?

2 'Crackle' is an example of what poetic device? What does it tell you about the attitude of the thistle?

3 What does the use of alliteration in 'A revengeful burst of resurrection' help suggest? Look up the word 'resurrection' in a dictionary. What is the poet suggesting about the way this plant keeps coming back?

4 List the metaphors in the poem that suggest the plant is full of aggression.

5 Hughes characterises them as coming from the cold North, like Vikings, pale of hair and sharp and spiky. Why is this particularly appropriate?

6 What might he have in mind when referring to 'the underground stain of a decayed Viking'?

7 What does 'the gutturals of dialects' suggest about their place and status in the plant kingdom?

8 Any attempt at mowing them down is to them a 'feud'. What is suggested by this word?

9 In the last verse in what ways do they display human characteristics?

10 The poem ends by using a tone that seems deliberately flat and down-to-earth. Why?

Themes

What does the poem have to say about the
following themes?

▸ the resilience of nature
▸ the relationship between nature and humankind?

Links with other Poems

This poem is linked to 'Nettles', as they both
describe stinging plants that fight back when
under attack.

WRITING BASED ON THE POEM

Imagine that a recently independent country has decided to adopt a plant,
vegetable or flower as its emblem. Choose one and write a speech to
persuade the government to adopt your choice.

'Trout'

BY SEAMUS HEANEY

Before Reading

Discuss in pairs, or as a class:

✱ What possible reasons might a poet have for wanting to write about a trout?

✱ If you were writing about one how would you see it?

Exploring the Poem

In pairs, discuss and make brief notes in response to the following questions.

Language and Style

1. Were you surprised by the way that Heaney describes the trout?
   If so, why?

2. In the first verse Heaney describes the trout, on the one hand, as like a
   'fat gun-barrel', and, on the other, as slipping 'like butter down the
   throat of the river'. What is he trying to convey?

3 Trace the pattern of images used by Heaney throughout the poem to capture the power of the trout. Most of them are metaphorical and concerned with what?

4 Ask yourself, in each above example, what the poet is trying to put across.

5 Would you agree that the poet is very economical with words and yet has a lively and energetic style? Suggest the ways he achieves this. Look closely at some examples of the way words are fitted to the poet's purpose.

6 In the third verse what does the poet suggest by saying the trout 'is fired' (rather than 'fires itself')?

7 Does this poem make any statement about human beings? If so, how?

8 Comment on the last two lines of the fourth verse. Why 'never burnt out'? What does 'cold blood' suggest?

9 What effect is achieved by having the last line standing by itself?

Themes

What does the poem have to say about the trout in terms of:
- ▶ where it lives
- ▶ how it is adapted to its environment
- ▶ its character
- ▶ its power.

Links with other Poems

This poem is linked to 'Mushrooms', as they both describe the unexpected power of living things we see only as food. Like 'The Stag' it is the lord of its own element – until humans come along.

WRITING BASED ON THE POEM

Heaney uses the attributes of a gun to describe the trout. Try writing a poem or piece of description using an extended metaphor.

Here are some suggestions:
- ▶ a cat as a sports car
- ▶ a tree as a house.

Nature and Change

> **POEMS WITHIN *NATURE* THAT DEAL WITH THE THEME OF NATURE AND CHANGE**
>
> 'Iguana Memory' by Grace Nichols
> 'Keeping Orchids' by Jackie Kay
> 'Nettles' by Vernon Scannell
> 'The Flowers' by Selima Hill
> 'The Five Students' by Thomas Hardy
> 'A Blade of Grass' by Brian Patten

'Iguana Memory'

BY GRACE NICHOLS

Before Reading

Discuss in pairs, or as a class:

✱ The poet remembers seeing an iguana, a kind of lizard that lives in trees, when she was very small. Do you have any very early memories of seeing an unusual creature? What did you feel at the time?

✱ What do you think you would feel now if an iguana suddenly popped up in your back garden or some local place?

Exploring the Poem

In pairs, discuss and make brief notes in response to the following questions.

Language and Style

1 The poem begins as a child might, leaving out the pronoun 'I' and plunging straight into the verb; and confusing tenses, moving from the past 'saw' to the present 'came'. Why do you think the poet writes in this way? (See the glossary note for **verb** on page 9.)

2 We often speak of leaves rustling – so how appropriate is the onomatopoeic word here?

3 It was 'green like moving newleaf sunlight': how does this convey that the reptile is part of its sunny, leafy environment? What kind of figure of speech has been used?

4 The poet uses another comparison, which is less poetic and rather more direct and literal. What is it? How does it help to suggest that the 'voice', here, is the child's own? What is the effect of 'so it seemed to me'?

5 Consider how the language of the last four lines has a more mature feel to it. Why is this?

6 What do the child and the reptile have in common?

7 The poem has no punctuation. Does this make it easier or harder to understand? Suggest reasons why Grace Nichols chose to write in this way.

Themes

What does the poem have to say about the following themes?
  ▶ the significance of early memories
  ▶ the innocence of childhood.

Links with other Poems

This poem links with 'Roe-Deer', as they both describe a brief moment's eye contact with another species, before the creature goes scurrying off.

WRITING BASED ON THE POEM

Write about an encounter with nature that you remember from your early childhood, which perhaps you failed to understand at the time but saw the significance of later.

'Keeping Orchids'

BY JACKIE KAY

Before Reading

Discuss in pairs, or as a class:

✳ Jackie Kay was adopted at birth and only found her birth mother in later life. How would it feel to be in this position?

✳ Would it be better not to meet? Discuss this difficult question.

✳ Imagine you are adopted. What might your adoptive parents feel about you meeting your birth mother?

Exploring the Poem

This is a poem which works largely through symbols – images that seem to carry hidden meanings, which become obvious when you think about them. In pairs, discuss and make brief notes in response to the following questions.

Language and Style

1 How does the first line set out to be deliberately difficult to understand?

2 Why does she carry the orchids home 'like a baby in a shawl'? What parallel is being suggested?

3 Does she value them because they symbolise her first meeting with her mother? Or is there a note of bitterness because they are the only present her mother has ever given her?

4 It seems some orchids have not yet opened out. What does this symbolise?

5 Her mother's face is 'fading fast' and her voice is going away as though down a tunnel. Why is the poet having difficulty in maintaining a vivid memory?

6 Why might her mother have made contact after the years of neglect? Does the poet believe she is being used as some kind of replacement? For what?

7 Do you detect a double meaning in 'my mother's hands are all I have'?

8 Comment on the bitter irony of 'A bag of tricks'. What does this tell us of her view of her mother?

9 At the end is the poet considering deliberately cutting herself off from her mother? Is this being symbolised by 'cutting the stems with a sharp knife'? Why would this be ironical?

Themes

What does the poem have to say about the following themes?
  ▶ the symbolic qualities of flowers
  ▶ the link between a mother and her child.

Links with other Poems

This poem is linked to 'Flowers' as both describe the relationship between a parent and a daughter, and use flowers as symbols.

WRITING BASED ON THE POEM

Write the letter a person in the poet's position might write to their birth mother, setting out their thoughts and feelings about their relationship.

'Nettles'

BY VERNON SCANNELL

Before Reading

Discuss in pairs, or as a class:

✱ Why do plants *arm* themselves? Is it just to stop humans from uprooting them?

✱ Try to work out a good definition for weeds, which will show how they are different from other *proper* plants and flowers.

✱ Why, in general, do we seem to disapprove of weeds?

Exploring the Poem

In pairs, discuss and make brief notes in response to the following questions.

Language and Style

1 Scannell sees the nettles in military terms. List the metaphors he uses to capture their fighting nature.

2 How does the poet try to make us feel sympathy for his son?

3 What tells us that the poet attempts to control his anger, and how do we know that he does not succeed?

4 In several of his poems, Scannell makes reference to World War I. Is there any hint in this poem about the effects of war?

5 In what sense are the nettles seen as symbolic of life itself? What might his son have learned from them?

6 Comment on the rhyme scheme used by the poet, and how effective it is in a poem of this type. (See the glossary note for **rhyme scheme** on page 17.)

Themes

What does the poem have to say about the following themes?
- how nature reinforces and renews itself
- the poet's attitude to his son
- what the poet learned from the experience
- what he hoped his son would learn.

Links with other Poems

This poem links very obviously with 'Thistles', and also with those poems that suggest it is impossible to try to tame or contain nature's force, for example 'Wind'.

WRITING BASED ON THE POEM

Find out what we mean when we speak of 'grasping the nettle', if you don't know already. Write about an incident when you had to do just that.

'The Flowers'

BY SELIMA HILL

Before Reading

Discuss in pairs, or as a class:

* Why do we put flowers around graves? Do they symbolise anything or are they there just for pretty decoration?

* In graveyards, you often see graves that appear to be badly neglected. Is this a sign of disrespect for the dead – or might there be other reasons?

* These days far more people in this country are cremated rather than buried. Why is this? Which do you think is best, and why?

Exploring the Poem

In pairs, discuss and make brief notes in response to the following questions.

Language and Style

1 In the first verse, it seems the daughter has more drive, determination and organisation than the mother when it comes to attending to the grandfather's grave. Pick out the active verbs that suggest this.

2 Notice the simile 'swaying like a candle-bearer'. It has suggestions, perhaps, of someone in church bearing the votive candle, symbolising the fulfilment of a vow. What is the poet getting at here about the girl's relationship with her grandfather?

3 What simile does the poet use to describe herself? Are any feelings of guilt suggested in it?

4 What evidence is there of neglect of the grave in the second verse? Although the tone of the description is rather matter-of-fact is there any suggestion the poet is feeling guilty?

5 Is it because the love someone has for a father is different from that for a grandfather, that the two females act differently?

6 What might be implied in the daughter's statement: 'It's finished now'? Could it be that the poet's grief will never end, whereas her daughter's will be rather more short-lived?

7 Discuss the symbolism of the final image of the two females riding home together 'moving apart and coming together again'. What might the 'ruts' represent?

Themes

What does the poem have to say about the following themes?
▶ attitudes, in general, to a) death, b) nature
▶ the feelings of the young for the old.

Links with other Poems

This poem links with 'A Blade of Grass', as they both describe how older people lose sight of the significance of a simple symbol of nature, which younger people can appreciate.

WRITING BASED ON THE POEM

Write the child's version of this *story*, using your imagination to fill in the details of the mother's relationship with the grandfather.

'The Five Students'

BY THOMAS HARDY

Before Reading

Discuss in pairs, or as a class:

* Imagine both of you and three of your friends in ten years' time. How will you have changed? Where will you be? Who will be the most ambitious?

* Now project yourselves forward another forty years. Who is likely to be the most successful? The richest? The happiest?

Exploring the Poem

In pairs, discuss and make brief notes in response to the following questions.

Language and Style

1 Is Hardy really talking about five students who went to school or college together? He may well be, but what might he also have in mind?

2 What might he have in mind when he says 'strenuously we stride'?

3 Trace the allegory through the poem. Each verse represents a different age of man. Explain how Hardy depicts life as a journey through the seasons of the year.

4 Discuss the rhyme and rhythm. What contribution does the general regularity and smoothness make to the poem's meaning?

5 The poet uses 'beating' and 'stalk': two words that are used in hunting. What is he trying to suggest?

6 It seems it is the old who are the stalkers. What is he stalking?

7 Comment on the use Hardy makes of natural imagery throughout the poem.

8 Suggest reasons why he uses capital letters for 'He' and 'She'.

9 Look up the word 'anon' in a dictionary. It is also short for 'anonymous'. Explain the pun that Hardy is making.

Themes

What does the poet have to say about the following themes?
  ▶ the ways in which we change as we grow older
  ▶ his own attitude to growing old.

Links with other Poems

This poem links with those poems which suggest that people lose their empathy with green nature as they grow old, e.g. 'A Blade of Grass'.

WRITING BASED ON THE POEM

Write a series of diary entries, many years apart, to show how a person's feelings and perceptions change as they grow old.

'A Blade of Grass'

BY BRIAN PATTEN

Before Reading

Discuss in pairs, or as a class:

✳ When two people are in a relationship what do they usually give each other as a token of their feelings?

✳ If you were offered a blade of grass what would be your reaction? Would you approve? Or be offended? Or take it as a joke?

✳ If the other person insisted it was a serious and well-meant present, could you see the point they were making? What present would you give in return?

Exploring the Poem

In pairs, discuss and make brief notes in response to the following questions.

Language and Style

1 She has asked for a poem and been offered instead a blade of grass. How convincing is his 'this ... will do'? Is it supposed to be convincing?

2 How does he attempt to justify the present by saying having 'dressed itself in frost', it's better than any poetic image he could create?

3 What point is he trying to make about nature and art?

4 What does he mean by 'immediate'? What form does it exist in, that a poem does not?

5 She is not convinced but has toned down her earlier not 'good enough' with 'not quite'. What does this suggest?

6   Do we sympathise with her? Has she got a good point?

7   Why does he call the poem that he eventually decides to write 'a tragedy'? Is he being ironic and suggesting that it's far from tragic? Or is he being completely serious – and suggesting what?

8   Why should it be increasingly difficult as we grow older to be offered or receive a simple blade of grass? Discuss the question not as a literal statement, but one with symbolic meaning.

9   Is 'accept' meant to be a pun? (Consider the difference between accepting a gift and accepting an idea.)

10 There is only one metaphor. Find it in the second verse. Why is this lack of figurative imagery effective – and what prominence does it give to the main symbol?

11 This poem is an example of free verse, that is, it does not rhyme and it has not got a regular rhythm. Why is this a particularly appropriate form for the subject matter? (See the glossary note for **free verse** on page 14.)

Themes

What does the poem have to say about the following themes?
> the relationship between the poet and the girl
> nature's superiority to art
> symbols of beauty or love
> the materialism (being 'into' possessions) that comes increasingly as you get older
> there also is a hint of the age-old theme of the natural cycle of change shared by all life-forms. We grow old, we die, we return to earth – where the blades of grass grow.

Links with other Poems

This poem links to several poems, already named – and to 'Iguana Memory', as both are about the loss of natural simplicity that comes as we grow older.

WRITING BASED ON THE POEM

Using your imagination of the event on which this poem might have been based, write a playscript or a piece of dialogue about the conversation between the two people. (See the glossary note for **dialogue** on page 21.)

Preparing for the Exams

As you can see from the examples of practice questions below, you will often be asked to select one of the poems yourself in the exam. This is a skill you need to practise because if you make a poor choice, you may lose valuable time.

To help you to select suitable poems quickly try this activity. Don't allow yourself more than a minute to make your selection (only choose from the collection you are studying):

Choose a Poem

In Such a Time as This

Find a poem that describes a place vividly.

Identity

Find a poem that deals with ethnic identity.

Nature

Find a poem that tells a story.

When you have chosen your poem, compare it with poems chosen by others. Do you all agree? Are some poems more suitable than others?

Now test each other. In pairs, take it in turns to 'find a poem that ...'

EXAM PRACTICE QUESTIONS

In Such a Time as This

Higher Tier

Look again at 'Yellow' and ONE other poem from **Childhood Memories**.
How do the poets bring these experiences to life?
Support your answer with reference to the texts.

Foundation Tier

Look again at 'Brendon Gallacher' and at ONE other poem from *In Such a Time as This*.

How do the writers of these two poems help you to understand the events or incidents they describe?

For each poem, you should write about:
- ▶ the feelings of the people
- ▶ the events that took place
- ▶ the poet's use of language.

You should support your answer with examples from each text.

Identity

Higher Tier

Consider how the poets in 'Once Upon a Time' and 'Still I Rise' explore the meaning of freedom.
Support your answer with examples from the texts.

Foundation Tier

Look again at 'Follower' and 'Once Upon a Time'. How do the poets show the relationships between the fathers and their sons?

You should explain:
- ▶ the relationship as shown in 'Follower'
- ▶ the relationship as shown in 'Once Upon a Time'
- ▶ the language used by each poet.

Support your answer with examples from the texts.

Nature

Higher Tier

Look again at 'The Thought-Fox' and 'A Blade of Grass'. Explain how both poets view writing poetry and their relationship with the subject matter.
Support your answers with examples from the texts.

Foundation Tier

Look again at 'The Stag' and 'Roe-Deer', also by Hughes. Discuss how both poems show the 'secret' and 'private' world of the animals being disturbed by humans.

Show how each poem:
- ▶ describes the animals in their natural environment
- ▶ shows the effect of humans on the animals.

2 Non-fiction Prose

The Specifications

English A (1203)

THE CRAFT OF THE WRITER

Paper 2F (Foundation Tier) or 4H (Higher Tier)
Section B: Non-fiction texts in *The Edexcel Anthology for GCSE English*

One question will be set based on close reading of the prepared non-fiction texts in *The Edexcel Anthology for GCSE English*, showing sustained interpretation of content, language and presentation. The question will focus on one named extract from the selection.

Assessment Objectives

You are required to demonstrate the ability to read with insight and engagement, making appropriate references to texts and developing and sustaining interpretations of them. You are further required to understand how writers use linguistic, structural and presentational devices to achieve their effects, and to comment on the ways language varies and changes.

This unit focuses on the Non-fiction Prose section of the *Edexcel Anthology*, which consists of a range of non-fiction texts arranged in three categories:

- literary non-fiction
- a group of newspaper articles on the theme of 'Sport For All'
- a group of newspaper articles on the theme of 'Parents and Children'.

The first category should be read in much the same way as you would read a short story. In other words, although the writers are relating real experiences, their aim is similar to that of a writer of fiction: to entertain the reader and to make their writing as vivid and powerful as possible.

The second and third categories require a very different kind of reading. These are newspaper articles that put forward opinions and points of view. The readers want to persuade you to their opinion and, although they may have some personal experience of the subject, these are not personal accounts.

Before you start reading properly flip through the Non-fiction Prose section of the *Edexcel Anthology* and see if you can spot the important differences. Look at layout, language (tenses, vocabulary), style and tone.

Literary Non-fiction

'Mongolian Wedding'

BY STANLEY STEWART

Before Reading

Stanley Stewart was born in Ireland but raised in Canada. He writes regularly about travel in broadsheet newspapers and has won many awards for his travel books. This passage is taken from an account of a thousand-mile horseback ride from Istanbul across the mountains and deserts of Central Asia, which formed the old Mongol Empire of Ghengis Khan. It was a journey full of amazing encounters, with amazing people – as you will see from the 'boisterous occasion', the Mongolian wedding.

'Mongolian Wedding' belongs to the non-fiction **genre** (or type) of travel writing. Most modern travel books (not to be confused with travel guides) set out to describe places, people and culture in a way that is informative, entertaining and amusing.

Here is an extract from a travel website. With a partner, discuss the following features:

 ▶ the purpose of the writing
 ▶ the audience
 ▶ the style, especially the use of adjectives.

Glossary

Genre: is the word for a type or category of literature.

The greenest and certainly the best known of the Ionian Islands, Corfu has attracted admirers for centuries – indeed this was Homer's 'beautiful and rich land'.

The air is often scented from the herbs and wild flowers that proliferate on this garden island and the mountainous interior is further adorned with slender cypress trees, olive groves and villages. In fact so varied and colourful is the landscape and so welcoming the people that this is one of the best Greek islands to explore, especially on foot. The timeless rhythm of agricultural life has changed little and verdant, fertile valleys – such as the great vale of Ropa – still yield a rich harvest.

Those developed resorts that there are, are well contained and the most part of the island is fringed with stunning coastal scenery, golden sands and clear blue waters. Many of the established tourist centres are to the north of Corfu Town but it is also here that you will find some of the most beautiful and unsullied stretches of coastline of the entire island, and delightful villages beneath the slopes of the mighty Mount Pantokrator – the island's highest peak (906m). Visit Strinylas and Nisaki as well as the village of Kalami where the Brothers Durrell spent so much of their time and where they were inspired to write many of their books.

The island's obvious beauty has shaped its history for it has been fought over by almost any nation to have ever taken up arms – from the Romans to Napoleon, Russia and of course, the British. Corfu Town, the island's capital, best illustrates these many occupying influences. French-style arcaded buildings flank a green esplanade and cricket pitch. Georgian mansions and Byzantine churches complete the picture. The delightful old town, wedged between two vast fortresses is perhaps more reminiscent of Venice than Greek towns.

Present day Corfu is an excellent destination for families, adventurers and sport lovers alike and manages to condense all that characterises the Ionian Islands.

Language note: a cliché is a well-known, well-used expression e.g. 'the sparkling sea and sand'. Can you find any examples in this text?

Exploring the Text

Travel writing, however, is very different from the writing in travel websites and brochures.

Stanley Stewart:
> uses himself as a first-person narrator
> is interested in people, their emotions and culture
> describes places that are remote and often unglamorous and dangerous
> uses original language, often of a literary kind
> aims to amuse and educate the reader.

✱ What sort of reader is 'Mongolian Wedding' aimed at?

Tone

The tone of this passage is humorous and light-hearted. It makes use of irony and is slightly exaggerated. The tone is set in the first paragraph, where it is ironical that the wedding guests apologise for their bad behaviour in advance and warn about others, and then admit they, themselves, are as bad.

We recognise the tone is not serious, and the use of irony, because anyone who knows that they are going to do something wrong, should be able to avoid it. Whether we are amused or not depends on context. Because we sense that no real harm will occur, we are amused.

✷ With a partner, look for other examples of irony in the passage, list them and explain them.

For the sake of humour, Stewart has probably used exaggeration here and there – to produce a series of cartoon-like images, e.g. 'The bride's elder sister, shrugging off all assistance, fell headfirst from the tailgate, bounced twice and came to rest, smiling, against a door post.'

✷ Discuss the use the author makes of the **caricature** of 'Wyatt Earp', in lines 85–110:
   ▶ for humour
   ▶ as a convenient label
   ▶ to draw a parallel.

✷ Find and discuss two or three other examples of humour. Discuss and explain how the author achieves this effect.

✷ Consider whether Stanley Stewart is making any serious points about the following themes:
   ▶ human nature in general
   ▶ the absurdity of marriage rituals and ceremonies
   ▶ Mongolian people and culture.

If so, what are they? Write a paragraph on each, explaining the point and backing up your views with examples from the text.

Glossary

Caricature: It is a cartoon-like exaggeration of a person.

Language

Stewart's language is lively, interesting and energetic, without using too much in the way of metaphors and similes, or other figurative expressions.

Notice some of the features of his style:

▷ variation of sentence length
▷ relatively straightforward vocabulary
▷ occasional use of Mongolian nouns to add realism, or humour
▷ sparing but effective use of adjectives.

WRITING ACTIVITY

1. Look back at the extract from the Corfu travel brochure and compare it with 'Mongolian Wedding'.
   Which text enables us to learn more about a foreign culture?
   Support your views with evidence from the texts.

2. The author gives us a taste of the atmosphere of a Mongolian wedding. Imagine you are a Mongolian local journalist sent to cover this wedding reception. Write it up as a news item, inventing suitable names for the characters. You may care to include the following:
   ▷ the fight between the two families
   ▷ descriptions of the bride, groom and others
   ▷ an interview with the foreign writer, Stanley Stewart, about his impressions.

Write it up using a headline, sub-headings and the presentational features of a newspaper.

A group of young Mongolian dancers in national costume

'The Other Side of the Dale'

BY GERVASE PHINN

Before Reading

Gervase Phinn has written two best-selling **autobiographical** accounts of his experiences as a schools' inspector in North Yorkshire. This passage, from 'The Other Side of the Dale', tells of a visit to Barton Moor Parochial School, in his first year as an inspector.

✽ Discuss with a partner what effect you think the presence of an inspector has on a classroom.

Exploring the Text

Tone

✽ Write down any of the following words that fit the *tone* of this passage. (Look up in a dictionary any words that you do not know.)

Support your views with examples from the text.

acerbic	bitter	light-hearted
analytical	controversial	nostalgic
anecdotal	droll	persuasive
angry	farcical	poetic
argumentative	humorous	whimsical

✽ Look at the third paragraph (lines 10–15). Read it out a couple of times, and then try writing it out as if it is a poem in free verse. It has been started for you below.

From the classroom window,
The cold bleak moor stretched before us,
Strange and desolate.

✽ When you've finished, underline the metaphors in red, and label any other features of poetry you've noticed, e.g. alliteration or onomatopoeia.

✽ Read it out again, this time as poetry. Discuss the reasons why the author chose to put in this rather poetic paragraph. What kind of tone does it establish?

Glossary

Autobiography/ Autobiographical: the author's account of his or her own life.

Viewpoint

Two questions that may by now have occurred to you are:

1 How do we know this is non-fiction?

2 In what way is it different from an autobiographical novel?

One of the differences between this type of non-fiction and a novel is the narrator. In a novel, the narrator is either a character speaking in the first person, or the *voice* of someone who has seen everything that is going on. In autobiography, the author and the narrator are one and the same. The viewpoint, then, is how the narrator sees things and uses his material.

✳ What clues do we get to Gervase Phinn's character and viewpoint from his own writing? Write down everything you learn of him. Support your views with examples from the text.

Humour

The passage has a good deal of gentle humour, for example, the description of Mrs Durdon (lines 95–99) looking like a penguin.

✳ Find other examples of humour and discuss why they are funny.

Characters

✳ The chief characters in this passage are the Headteacher, Miss Sally Precious, and an 11-year-old pupil, Joseph Richard Barclay. Discuss them in detail.

✳ How does the author to a large extent let them characterise themselves in their speech, the language they use and the things they talk about?

✳ Try acting out the things they say. Are they realistic or are they caricatures?

Language

✳ Who is the author describing in the following quotations:

'. . . like a great mother hen gathering up her chicks.'

'He sat sober-faced at the front desk like the receptionist at a funeral parlour.'

'. . . explaining that she was on yard duty that morning, waddled off in the direction of the small playground.'

✳ Comment on the language and its comic effect.

✳ Rewrite in standard English the Yorkshire Dales' dialect that occurs in lines 62–70. What is the effect of this dialect?

✳ Look at how the author uses language to characterise Joseph in this passage, and discuss the questions in the boxes.

Why is this a suitable word in the circumstances?

What is the effect of this repetition?

What is the effect of putting these similar sounding words?

I stared for a moment at my companion. He was a strangely old-fashioned looking boy of about eleven, with a curiously old-fashioned way of speaking. Eleven-year-olds generally do not use words like 'perished' and 'skirmish' and 'pursued'. His hair was of the short-back-and-sides variety, a style that I had sported when I had been his age and he wore long grey trousers, a hand-knitted grey pullover, long grey stockings and sensible shoes. He could have been a schoolboy of the 1950s. Miss Precious's precocious pupil, no doubt.

'Well,' he said suddenly, 'I must get on. I have to collect the register. If you'll excuse me.'

Why does the author quote these three words?

Who does this kind of language remind us of?

Presentation

Discuss the author's use of quoted material (a poem and historical extracts) to make his account easier on the eye and more interesting to read.

SPEAKING & LISTENING

This passage is from the sort of autobiographical writing that is hugely popular. Do some research on the genre, possibly considering the popularity of the James Herriot vet books and the television series, *All Creatures Great and Small*.

Discuss in pairs, or as a class:

▶ the type of people most likely to read them

▶ why they have appeal

▶ your own opinion of them

▶ if Gervase Phinn's books would be interesting and entertaining to you (base your judgements not only on the subject matter of the extract but also its style and language).

WRITING ACTIVITIES

1. Imagine you are a schools' inspector visiting your school. Write an account of your first day, in a similar light, witty, autobiographical style to that of Gervase Phinn.

   Then write an evaluation of your piece, explaining what features of Gervase Phinn's style you have used, and how effectively you have captured it.

2. Imagine Miss Precious has to write a report on Joseph Barclay for his next school. Write this report describing him, his characteristics, abilities and achievements.

   Try to sum him up in about 50 words.

'The Lady in the Van'

BY ALAN BENNETT

Before Reading

Use the Internet to research a little about Alan Bennett. You'll probably find him an interesting character – he is the author of *Talking Heads*, a series of witty but penetrating monologues, and of the play that was later made into the film *The Madness of King George*.

Exploring the Text

Content

This passage is taken from *Writing Home*, a loose collection of diaries, autobiographical essays and anecdotes by Alan Bennett.

It's about:

▶ Miss Shepherd, a strange but likeable old lady.

▶ In 1971, Alan allowed her to park her van in his drive.

▶ She continued to live in it for the next 15 years to her death.

Style

As is very often the case in this type of autobiographical non-fiction, the tone is humorous and it is also compassionate. We are invited to laugh at the old lady but gently and sympathetically. The author also pokes fun at himself.

One obvious example of humour is the episode where Vincent Price, the actor famous for his roles in horror movies (and pictured playing the lead role in *Diary of a Madman*), is told to 'Pipe down'.

✱ Explain the humour in the words 'Pipe down', which comes from the situation and context. Try to find other examples of situation humour.

The author uses gentle irony throughout the passage. Consider, for example, this expression: 'a manoeuvre which once again enabled her to go through her full repertoire of hand signals'.

✱ Discuss this in its context. Why is it moderately funny?

When the writer, in apparent seriousness, says the opposite of what you would reasonably expect, it is known as irony.

This expression is ironical because:
- ▶ She was only driving a few yards.
- ▶ She did not really need handsignals at all, certainly not her full repertoire.

✳ What do we learn of her character from this small incident?

Consider another example: 'Though I think me being an older person he knew I would be more responsible. Though not all old ladies perhaps.'

✳ Read lines 34–43 and put the above quotation in its context. In the light of what we know of her, why would the chemist be unlikely to think her 'responsible'? Why is it ironical?

✳ Notice how Bennett uses the present tense in the diaries, e.g. 'I am working in the garden'; 'She tells me', and so on. What effect does this have?

Characters

'She was middle-class and spoke in a middle-class way, though her querulous and often resentful demeanour tended to obscure this; it wasn't a gentle or a genteel voice. Running through her vocabulary was a streak of schoolgirl slang' (lines 64–68).

✳ In groups, discuss Miss Shepherd.
- ▶ What kind of lady was she?
- ▶ What can we tell of her from the way she dressed? Her habits and interests?
- ▶ Do we agree that she might have been a nun if she 'could have had more modern clothes, longer sleep and better air'?
- ▶ Why do you think someone middle class and well spoken would choose to live in this way?

✳ Use your imagination to write three of Miss Shepherd's diary entries. Spread them out over a period and refer to things that happened in the passage.
　▶ Try to capture her thoughts about other people, in particular the author.
　▶ Try to capture her way of speaking.

✳ Discuss in groups the episode of a well-known author allowing a destitute old woman to live in his garden.
　▶ Was he wise to do this?
　▶ What were his possible motives?
　▶ What impressions of him do we gain overall?
　▶ Would you have done the same?

Language

You can tell the author is writing for adults by his large and mature vocabulary. He uses, for example:

▶ 'manoeuvre' and 'repertoire'

▶ 'scrutinized' and 'sojourn'

▶ 'querulous' and 'demeanour'

Look up these words in a dictionary if you don't understand them and any others in the passage you don't know.

These words have an ironical purpose. They are there to set a serious and solemn tone that is on a different level from the subject matter – a shabbily dressed old woman with a bad hygiene problem! The gap between the two levels is the irony and the humour.

Bennett also uses more informal words and expressions like 'midden' and 'nightie' and 'her Charlie Brown pitcher's hat'.

✳ What is the effect of this mixed vocabulary? Do you think he has got the balance right, bearing in mind his audience?

✳ Would it have been better with more informal and **colloquial** expressions and fewer difficult ones?

✳ List examples of words and phrases you find interesting and say why they are effective.

Glossary

Colloquial language: is close to the spoken variety. It is informal with a chatty tone.

Imagery and Word-Pictures

Notice the comparison between the handbrake and the sword Excalibur – which by legend was stuck in the stone before being freed by the future King Arthur.

✱ Why does the author make such a comparison?

Bennett uses a series of images to describe Miss Shepherd:
 ▶ 'spectral figure' (line 25)
 ▶ 'lying on her side like an effigy on a tomb' (line 26)
 ▶ 'like an animal that has been disturbed' (line 28)
 ▶ 'Miss S. sits at the door of the van slowly turning over the contents of the box like a chimpanzee' (lines 89–90).

✱ What do they collectively suggest? Is this an effective way of describing her?

Layout

✱ Comment on how Bennett finds ways of varying the format to make it more interesting, for example:
 ▶ The first 30 lines are in the form of a conventional autobiography.
 ▶ We then have four diary-type entries taken from a period of over 19 months.
 ▶ The *May 1976* entry contains a conversation appearing in playscript form.

✱ What is the overall effect of breaking the text up in this way?

✱ Is it an effective way of relating Miss Shepherd's story?

✱ When it moves to diary form, do you think it becomes more or less interesting?

SPEAKING & LISTENING

Write and deliver a monologue in which Miss Shepherd describes her trip to the seaside with the other old people. Make it witty and imaginative. (It might help if you could see an excerpt from *Talking Heads*; the video is published by BBC Worldwide Publishing.)

WRITING ACTIVITY

What impression do we get of Miss Shepherd's opinion of authority from her conversation (lines 78–88) with the social worker? Imagine and compose another conversation between the two that might have occurred when the social worker tried to persuade Miss Shepherd to go into an old people's home. Try to capture both parties' ways of speaking, and their point of view in your writing.

'Don't Leave me Here to Die'

BY CATHY O' DOWD

Before Reading

'Don't Leave me Here to Die' is taken from *Just for the Love of it*. Cathy O'Dowd (pictured), a South African, was the first woman to climb Mount Everest from both sides, once via the South Col route, in 1996, and again via the North Ridge, in 1999. This extract tells of her failure, however, in 1998.

* In groups discuss the type of person who climbs mountains or does daring activities, and their reasons for doing this. Consider their possible motives:
  ▶ seeking excitement not available in ordinary lives in towns and cities
  ▶ pushing themselves to their limits to discover more about their capabilities
  ▶ showing their independence and seeking personal freedom.

Recently there has been an explosion of interest in so-called 'extreme' sports – base jumping, tow-in-surfing, street lugeing, and so on. Use the Internet to find out about these activities.

* Can you suggest reasons why such sports are becoming popular? What is your opinion on taking risks in the name of sport?

Exploring the Text

The extract is a serious, first-hand account of the second South African Everest expedition's attempt on the summit. It focuses on the **dilemma** experienced by the author, when encountering a severely injured female mountaineer.

* Read the first column of the extract. Write a short account (30–40 words) of what you think is Cathy O'Dowd's dilemma. You may care to begin with: 'Cathy O'Dowd's dilemma consisted of whether she should . . .'

* How effective do you think the opening paragraphs are at setting the scene, engaging your interest and creating a life-or-death situation? You may care to consider the tension and suspense the author creates by:
  ▶ referring to 'the body'
  ▶ describing the strange, jerking movement
  ▶ revealing there was little chance of saving the injured climber's life.

Glossary

Dilemma: It is a situation in which you have two choices, both of which have equally bad consequences. It is a 'no-win' situation.

Tone

The passage is full of brutal truths, e.g. 'Anyone who becomes immobile on a mountain as large and remote as Everest is probably going to die.'

✳ Go through the passage and find three more similar examples. What tone do these kind of expressions create?

✳ The extract has a completely humourless tone throughout. Suggest reasons why it has to be written in this way and why humour would be inappropriate.

Content

✳ Explain how Fran came to be in the position they found her in.

✳ Make a list of the possible reasons why it seemed pointless to try to take Fran back down the mountain.

✳ In the end, three of the South African party decide not to attempt to rescue Fran but also not to carry on themselves. What made them decide to give up?

✳ Why had Cathy in particular lost the will to reach the summit?

✳ Why are the last three paragraphs so important?

Characters

✳ This is an autobiographical work and the only character to fully emerge from the extract is the author herself. Consider her viewpoint. Do you agree that she is frank and honest about her feelings throughout the whole episode?

✳ What do the following quotations tell us about her?
  ▶ 'Should we throw it all away for some rescue attempt that was doomed?'
  ▶ 'Why not just turn away and climb on?'
  ▶ '"We can't just leave," I insisted.'
  ▶ 'For a shocked second, I felt as if I was glimpsing a possible future for myself.'

Language

Much of the language of this passage is functional and plain, e.g. 'Life lay in keeping moving, as that generated body heat and, with every metre of descent, moved you into thicker air' or, 'We had no capacity for giving her oxygen. Her mask would not fit our bottles. We carried spare bottles but no spare masks. For the oxygen to have any effect, she would have to be put on high flow, and stay on for hours.'

✳ Why is this kind of language particularly effective in this type of writing?

✳ How is it appropriate to the context?

✳ Why is it convincing and persuasive?

* There are, however, some examples of more figurative language, such as:
  ▶ '. . . it made her look like a porcelain doll.'
  ▶ 'She was as helpless as a rag doll.'
  ▶ '. . . as useless as strands of spaghetti.'

* What effect do these have?

Presentation

This extract is taken from a book that was set out in the standard page format.

* List and discuss the features of newspaper presentation that have been added.

* Do they improve the article's appeal, making it more attractive and readable?

SPEAKING & LISTENING

Organise a debate, considering whether you would have left Fran by herself. Half the class should be in favour of trying to bring her down the mountain; the other half should argue against it.

WRITING ACTIVITY

Imagine that when Cathy O'Dowd returned home, she had to write a letter to her sponsors thanking them for their help but explaining the reasons why the expedition was not completely successful. What reasons would she find and how would she explain them? Write the letter (remembering that two of her party made it to the top).

Newspaper Articles

The second and third categories within the Non-fiction Prose section of *The Edexcel Anthology for GCSE English* consist of linked newspaper articles. When looking at newspaper feature articles you need to be aware of the following questions:

What is the article's trigger?

▶ It will generally be stimulated by something topical.

Who is it written for?

▶ The audience will generally be the newspaper's readership – but some are a little more specific, e.g. for younger or older readers or for people with a particular interest. Look for clues as to who it is aimed at.

What is its purpose?

▶ Newspaper articles are written to inform, report, describe or instruct, but features are often intended in addition to entertain or persuade.

What is its tone?

▶ Is it serious and thoughtful?

▶ Does it use humour to make a serious point?

▶ Is it angry or hard-hitting?

▶ Does it attempt to shock in order to hit home?

What feelings does it arouse?

▶ Agreement?

▶ Disagreement?

▶ Not committed but recognise it has a point?

▶ Pleasure, sadness, annoyance, amazement?

What does it look like?

▶ Layout, fonts, print size, and so on.

▶ How do these contribute to the overall impression?

Who is it written by?

In a feature article, fact and opinion are often mixed to present a case and the writer's own point of view is perfectly clear.

▶ The writer might be an expert in the field.

▶ On the other hand, the writer might be an 'outsider', giving the commonsense view of a non-expert.

How does the writer come across?

▶ As friendly and informal?

▶ As distant and formal?

▶ As speaking on equal terms?

▶ As an expert teaching the less well-informed?

Clearly there are close connections here with tone, but the two are not always the same. A writer, for example, might be friendly and informal in manner and yet have a serious tone – or be distant and formal, but still use humour.

Does it succeed?

▶ If the way it is written interests the reader, it is – at least – effective.

▶ If the reader is persuaded or convinced by it, then the article is successful.

Sport For All

1 In small groups discuss sport in the school curriculum, using the following questions to help you:
   ▶ Why do we have it?
   ▶ Should it be compulsory?
   ▶ Should we have more or less of it?
   ▶ Should we take it more seriously and give it more support?

Each person should then write an approximately 100-word statement summing up their attitude to sport.

2 Use the Internet to do some research on the organisation, Sport England.
   ▶ Who is it run by?
   ▶ What are its aims?

Having heard what they have to say have you changed any of your views on sport?

'Save our Children from the Horrors of School Sport'

BY JOHN HARRIS

Before Reading

The trigger for John Harris's article is a survey released the previous day by Sport England, highlighting the reduction in P.E. time given to six- to eight-year-old children (Wendy Berliner's article, 'Mind Games', also refers to this). It was published in *The Independent*, an English broadsheet newspaper.

Use the Internet to briefly research what kind of newspaper *The Independent* is, and what kind of people read it.

Exploring the Text

Viewpoint

✱ Based on the first three paragraphs what do we learn of the author's attitude to the sports education he received at a young age?

✱ Why do you think he considers his own experiences are relevant (bearing in mind his audience)?

✱ Are his experiences in any way like your own?

Language

✱ Find the following examples of figurative language in the article and discuss them:
  ▶ 'ogre-like teachers'
  ▶ 'an unemployed vagrant'
  ▶ 'damp mornings spent responding to the yelps of borderline psychopaths'
  ▶ 'the England soccer team avoiding yet another early flight home'
  ▶ 'in ever-sensible Germany'.

✱ Translate each example into straightforward, literal English. Why are Harris's expressions much more effective? What tone does he achieve by using them? Can you find any other examples in the passage?

Tone

✳ Another feature of Harris's style is that he uses a good many colloquialisms. Some examples are:

  ▶ 'I cracked it'
  ▶ 'waffled on'
  ▶ 'Erm, not sure about that one, Trev.'

✳ How does this tone fit with any serious purpose the writer has?

SPEAKING & LISTENING

1 What do you imagine would be the games teacher's reaction to 'Team For A Laugh'?

2 Role-play what took place when he cancelled games for a full and frank discussion about the benefits of sport, and what he expected from his class.

Use the following characters:
  ▶ the teacher
  ▶ John Harris
  ▶ the talented young athlete slammed against the wall
  ▶ three or four athletic types
  ▶ three or four students that are not keen on sport.

WRITING ACTIVITIES

1 Imagine you are a games teacher who has read the article and felt moved to reply to it in the readers' letters section. Write a letter of approximately 250 words.

2 Write about the article, using the following questions and methods to help you:
  ▶ What kind of impression of the author have you formed so far?
  ▶ Summarise the arguments and conclusion.
  ▶ How has the author used language and presentation to put across the views?

Do the same for the other three articles within 'Sport For All' when you have studied them.

'School Sports Culture leads to Violence'

BY JULIAN BORGER

Before Reading

Julian Borger's article is from one of his weekly columns in *The Guardian*. His series of 'Washington D.C. dispatches' describes life in America from the point of view of an outsider. Note how he makes this clear when telling us 'The idea takes a little getting used to for an outsider.'

Use the Internet to briefly research what kind of newspaper *The Guardian* is, and who reads it.

Exploring the Text

The second column of writing begins by dealing with the issue of what happens to pupils who are not interested in, or not good at, sport.

✳ Discuss the fate of those not in the 'in group': the 'nerds' and the 'dweebs'.
  ▶ What happens to them?
  ▶ What is the attitude of teachers and administrators?
  ▶ What could be done to help them?

✳ Do you agree that the main part of Borger's article is introduced by this rhetorical question:

'If children who are good at sport are heroes, what does that make those who are not?'

Discuss this question in the light of what leads up to it and what follows.

One of the tricks of journalism (and persuasive writing in general) is to write in a way that seems to be **objective**, but which has disguised **subjective** elements. An example is given for you here:

OBJECTIVE STATEMENTS	SUBJECTIVE ELEMENTS
'It pits basketball teams from across the country against each other in a knockout tournament that is watched by tens of thousands of fans in huge sporting arenas and by tens of millions on television.'	The word 'huge' is subjective because it depends upon your viewpoint. In some sports a 10,000 crowd might be considered huge, but tiny in others. In the phrases, 'tens of thousands' and 'tens of millions', 'tens' is not objective, because there is no indication as to how many 'tens'.

✳ Find three other examples of apparently objective statements and point out any subjective elements, as above.

✳ Discuss the connotations of the following:
  ▶ 'March Madness'
  ▶ 'the annual Oxford-Cambridge boat race'
  ▶ 'the school "jocks"'
  ▶ 'the "in group"'
  ▶ 'nerds and dweebs'
  ▶ 'student-athlete'.

✳ Do they make the article easier or harder to understand?

✳ Discuss the impact of the last four paragraphs.
  ▶ What do we learn from them about the way American high schools recruit their sporting heroes?
  ▶ Why are some students taking a 'high risk'?
  ▶ Do these paragraphs provide an effective ending?

Glossary

Objective: judgements are unemotional and unbiased, describing an object as everybody would agree it really is.

Subjective: judgements involve personal views, with some bias, depending on your point of view.

SPEAKING & LISTENING

Discuss in groups, the issue of bullying in sport.
  ▶ Does the competitive nature of sport mean there will always be an element of bullying in it?
  ▶ What could be done to combat bullying?
  ▶ Is bullying a much wider issue than sport?
  ▶ Could the staff at the school do more to stop it?

WRITING ACTIVITY

Read the extract from the letter sent from a young reader to the *Los Angeles Times*, and reply to it, imagining that you are an American high school pupil who takes the opposite view.

'Mind Games'

BY WENDY BERLINER

Before Reading

'Don't be a couch potato!'

✻ In groups discuss how a person of your age should spend the six-week summer holidays. Try to work out an ideal programme, which would suit everybody and combine pleasure with all-round personal improvement.

✻ Afterwards the class should discuss each group's programme and try to decide which is the best. Do any of the programmes need to be modified?

Exploring the Text

✻ The third paragraph presents a view of why sport is good for you. In pairs, rewrite this paragraph, making the following changes:
  ▷ make its language more suitable for your age group
  ▷ get rid of 'jargon' (i.e. the specialised vocabulary).

✻ Is your version longer or shorter than the original? Is it easier to understand?

Viewpoint

✻ Do you agree that we learn next to nothing of Wendy Berliner from her writing? Note some features of her style:
  ▷ She never uses the pronoun 'I'.
  ▷ She writes in a serious and formal way, distancing herself from her subject and her readers.

✻ What is the effect of this and what impression do we form of her?

Style

Wendy Berliner writes in a style that you may not be familiar with. It is sometimes called an *academic* style because it is most frequently used by academics, i.e. university lecturers. One of the features of an academic style is that the writer tries to qualify every statement in an effort to be neutral, for example:
  ▷ '. . . a growing body of evidence *seems* to suggest . . .'
  ▷ 'This is *believed* to increase intelligence in mammals . . .'
  ▷ '. . . *appears* to be proving the link with academic feelings . . .'

✻ Do you find this style helpful or unhelpful?

✻ Would you prefer certainties rather than possibilities?

✻ What do you think of the conclusion that contains an 'If' and a 'might'? Should conclusions be more positive?

✻ Why, do you think, a writer chooses this style?

✻ Further features of this style are the use of:
  ▶ expert opinion
  ▶ surveys and research studies
  ▶ facts and figures
  ▶ jargon.

✻ Discuss how convinced you are by all of these features. Do you prefer this sort of 'meaty' article, full of research, or one where the writer gives his or her own impressions? Which style is the more effective, in your opinion, in dealing with a serious issue?

In groups, discuss how the ideas and findings in Wendy's article could be used to convince the American 'nerds and dweebs' to take more interest in sports.

Rewrite the article in a simpler and more 'punchy' way for teenagers.

You should:
  ▶ summarise the expert opinion
  ▶ use bullet points
  ▶ engage more with the reader.

'Sport in Schools'

BY DUNCAN MCNEIL MSP

Before Reading

This brief article is written by Duncan McNeil, a Member of the Scottish Parliament. It was published in the *Greenock Telegraph*, a Scottish evening newspaper.

✱ In groups work out questions to be used in a survey of what sport was like in school in past times. In a class discussion pick the best 5–10 questions (with no overlapping). Then use these to make a questionnaire.

✱ Each group should then target a particular age group from 30-year-olds to the 80-plus. The project should end with a full discussion of how sport in school has changed over the last 50 or 60 years.

Exploring the Text

Content

McNeil is making a single central assertion about the importance of Physical Education to today's schoolchildren. Try to summarise it in a single sentence.

Style

A feature of McNeil's style is to use colourful images to make his point, for example:

'Children are more likely to be managing Brazil on their Playstation than kicking a ball outside in the street.'

Rewritten in a straightforward style this would read:

'Children generally prefer computer-type games to playing sport in the street.'

* Find two other examples of colourful writing and 'translate' them in the same way.

* Why is McNeil's style more effective?

* Bearing in mind that McNeil is a politician, look at his final paragraph. In what ways is it like the style of a speech?

SPEAKING & LISTENING

How do McNeil's memories of sport in Scotland compare with John Harris's in England? What differences are there in the two writers' approaches and conclusions? Discuss in groups.

WRITING ACTIVITY

Write the speech Duncan McNeil might give in the Scottish Parliament outlining the measures being taken 'at every level' to encourage children to take part in school sports.

Parents and Children

This group of newspaper articles in the *Edexcel Anthology* deals with the relationship between parents and children, especially in relation to discipline. Before you read the anthology articles, think about your own views on the punishment of children.

✳ In groups, discuss whether there is any truth at all in the following well-known phrases:
   'Spare the rod and spoil the child'
   'Children should be seen and not heard'.

✳ What is your opinion of corporal punishment?

'Parents Learn How to Say NO'

BY ALEXANDRA FREAN

Before Reading

This article appeared in *The Times*. Use the Internet to briefly research what kind of newspaper this is, and who reads it.

Exploring the Text

Content

✳ Working in pairs, look up the word *liberal* in the dictionary.
   ▶ What does it mean as used in the passage?
   ▶ Who or what is the 'Liberal Generation'?
   ▶ Do you agree that their relaxed and tolerant attitude to childrearing has produced 'a generation of spoilt brats'?

Viewpoint

✳ What is Alexandra Frean's central assertion? Try to summarise it in a sentence.

SPEAKING & LISTENING

Debate the statement: 'Disciplining children through teaching and encouraging them is far more effective than corporal punishment.'

WRITING ACTIVITY

Write a playscript of the conversation between a teacher using the 'Stand and Think' method to counsel a pupil who had behaved in an aggressive and bullying manner.

'Pay your Children too much Attention . . .'

BY CHERRY NORTON

Before Reading

'Hot-housing' is a term applied to the method of intensively stimulating infant children's imagination in an effort to make them brighter and develop at a faster rate.

Discuss, in pairs, the following:
▶ A hot-house is another name for a greenhouse. Why is it appropriate here?
▶ Should children be allowed to develop at their own rate?
▶ Do they benefit from organised mental stimulation?

Exploring the Text

Viewpoint

Having considered the issue of 'hot-housing' are you surprised or not to read an expert opinion that it could 'lower children's curiosity, competence and ability to deal with the world on their own terms'?

Very often experts appear to get things wrong when it comes to passing judgements on human behaviour. One generation's experts are often flatly contradicted by the next generation.

* Consider the use of expert opinion in this article:
  ▶ Do we find it convincing?
  ▶ Would the article be better if it included some personal experience of parents?
  ▶ Should the author have given her own opinion?

* Now look back at the headline. In your opinion does it fairly represent Matthew Melmed's views?

SPEAKING & LISTENING

In groups, discuss the kind of educational toys and activities that, in your opinion, would be likely to stimulate a young child's brain without damaging side effects.

WRITING ACTIVITY

The manager of a toddler group has to write a letter to parents outlining the latest thinking on 'hot-housing'. Write her letter explaining either why the centre intends to carry on stimulating the children or why it has decided to stop it. Give reasons in simple terms and invite parents to comment.

'Use Persuasion not Coercion'

BY MADELEINE BUNTING

Before Reading

Consider in groups whether, in your opinion, a government has the *right* to pass a law against parents smacking their own young children, or the *obligation* to pass such a law.

Exploring the Text

Viewpoint

Notice how this writer, Madeleine Bunting, has immediately made her own position clear on the question of smacking.

* Look at the first paragraph.
  ▶ How effective is it?
  ▶ What kind of tone does it set for the rest of the article?
  ▶ Are we more comfortable with this kind of writer rather than one, like Wendy Berliner for example, who keeps her own opinions to herself?

* What is the point being made in the second paragraph?
  ▶ Do you agree that the child might grow up 'not really knowing what he or she wants'?
  ▶ Does this seem rather extreme to you?

* How effective is the last sentence as a conclusion? What possible connotations does the word 'help' have?

SPEAKING & LISTENING

The class should role-play a 'parenting class', where parents discuss their own experiences of controlling their children with a childcare expert, who is trying to convince them to 'use persuasion not coercion'. Some parents should be in favour of smacking, some against, and some not sure.

WRITING ACTIVITY

Compare and contrast the attitudes to discipline in the two articles 'Parents learn how to say no' and 'Use persuasion not coercion'. Also comment on the ways the authors put their ideas across.

'Smacking not the Answer, say Kids'

BY VARIOUS REPORTERS, *THE CHILDREN'S EXPRESS*

Before Reading

'Smacking not the Answer, say Kids' contains the views on corporal punishment of six teenagers from Northern Ireland. Discuss what their point of view is likely to be.

Exploring the Text

Viewpoint

The article is different from the three others in the unit, in that it gives children's views on the subject rather than adults', parents' and experts'.

* How do they compare with the views of your group as expressed in the discussion at the start of this section?

* Summarise the points made by Paul, Hugo, Sheena, Christopher, Thomas and Chris.

* Only Chris accepts that smacking is sometimes acceptable. What is your view on this?

* Discuss whether these children have got it about right.

* Are their views those of teenagers in general?

Style

The article was not produced by a journalist but by the children themselves.

* Consider how effective it is.

* Does it just rely on their experiences or are there any other persuasive points?

* What techniques of journalism have the children used?

WRITING ACTIVITIES

1. Imagine you work for the NSPCC, and have been asked to write a 500-word account of why the society supports a legal ban on smacking. It may help you to visit their website at **www.nspcc.org.uk**.

2. Tony Blair, the British Prime Minister, admitted to having occasionally smacked his first three children when they were little. Although he claimed he always afterwards regretted it, he said, 'there is a clear dividing line between administering discipline on the one hand and violence on the other'. Write a letter to Mr Blair either agreeing or disagreeing with his assessment and giving reasons why you do.

Preparing for the Exams

EXAM PRACTICE QUESTIONS

Higher Tier

Look again in the *Edexcel Anthology* at Stanley Stewart's account of a 'Mongolian Wedding' (from *In the Empire of Ghengis Khan*).

Discuss the ways in which Stewart creates a lively and amusing picture of marriage in a different culture. Comment on his use of language.

Foundation Tier

Look again in the *Edexcel Anthology* at Stanley Stewart's account of a 'Mongolian Wedding' (from *In the Empire of Ghengis Khan*).

What aspects of the wedding does he make both incredible and yet believeable?

You should consider:
- ▶ the setting and atmosphere
- ▶ the people present
- ▶ the language he uses.

Higher Tier

Look again in the *Edexcel Anthology* at Gervase Phinn's description of his visit to a school in the Yorkshire Dales.

How does Phinn make a visit to what is obviously an unusual school appeal to a wide audience? Comment on his use of language.

Foundation Tier

Look again in the *Edexcel Anthology* at Gervase Phinn's description of his visit to a school in the Yorkshire Dales.

What aspects of his visit did he find interesting and rewarding?

You should consider:
- ▶ the setting and atmosphere of the school
- ▶ the pupils and teachers
- ▶ the pupils' achievements and their use of language.

Higher Tier

Look again in the *Edexcel Anthology* at Alan Bennett's account of 'The Lady in the Van' (from *Writing Home*).

Discuss Bennett's attitude to the strange situation of having an old lady living in a van in his garden. Discuss his use of language and presentational features.

Foundation Tier

Look again in the *Edexcel Anthology* at Alan Bennett's account of 'The Lady in the Van' (from *Writing Home*).

What aspects of Miss Shepherd's life and character does he find unusual and/or amusing?

You should consider:
- ▶ the circumstances of her way of life
- ▶ her personality and attitude to other people
- ▶ the language she uses.

Higher Tier

Look again in the *Edexcel Anthology* at Cathy O'Dowd's account of finding an injured climber whilst attempting to reach the summit of Everest.

Discuss the problems that O'Dowd had to encounter and the way she makes her account vivid and gripping. Discuss her use of language.

Foundation Tier

Look again in the *Edexcel Anthology* at Cathy O'Dowd's account of finding an injured climber whilst attempting to reach the summit of Everest.

What aspects did O'Dowd find the most difficult and disturbing?

You should consider:
- ▶ the problems that arose as soon as the injured climber was found
- ▶ the setting and circumstances of the climb
- ▶ the way she gives her account, and her use of language.

Higher Tier

Look again at *two* of the articles in the *Edexcel Anthology*'s 'Sport for All' collection.

Comment on the way in which the writers put forward their views on school sports, making them persuasive and appealing.

Foundation Tier

Look again at *two* of the articles in the *Edexcel Anthology*'s 'Sport for All' collection.

Consider the writers' attitudes to the purpose and advantages of school sport.

You should comment on:
- their own experiences and/or the opinions of experts
- the way the subject is taught or should be taught
- the way they present their ideas and the language they use.

Higher Tier

Look again at *two* of the articles in the *Edexcel Anthology*'s 'Parents and Children' collection.

Comment in detail on the way the writers structure their articles to set out a case on how to bring up children in a disciplined way. Comment on their use of language.

Foundation Tier

Look again at *two* of the articles in the *Edexcel Anthology*'s 'Parents and Children' collection.

Comment on the different ways the writers argue in favour of persuasion being better than coercion in disciplining children.

You should comment on:
- the background to the debate that they introduce
- their own experiences and/or the opinions of experts
- the way they present their ideas and the language they use.

3 Different Cultures and Traditions

The Specifications

English B (1204)

THE CRAFT OF THE WRITER

Papers 2F (Foundation Tier) or 4H (Higher Tier)
Section B: Texts from Different Cultures and Traditions

There will be one question set, which will be assessed for reading, based on close reading of the prepared stories, showing sustained interpretation of content, language and presentation. You will be required to write about **two** of the pieces, at least one of which will be named.

Assessment Objectives

You are required to read with insight and engagement, making appropriate references to texts and developing and sustaining interpretations of them. You are further required to understand and evaluate how writers use linguistic, structural and presentational devices to achieve their effects, and to comment on the ways language varies and changes.

The speaking and listening activities in this unit are designed to enable you to satisfy the requirement for a drama-based assessment.

Note: Where the Texts from Different Cultures and Traditions are being used for coursework (Specification A), written work should address **at least two** short stories, and enable you to refer to others if desired. You will be expected to show an awareness of the cultural context of the works, and must make comments on the distinctive aspects of the texts.

This section of the *Edexcel Anthology* is set for examination in Specification B and Coursework in Specification A. It consists of a variety of short stories written by foreign authors, which reflect different cultures and traditions.

Before you start reading the stories, with a partner, consider the following statement:

All fiction tells the reader about the culture in which it was written.

Can you learn about a different culture from reading a story set within it? Think also about where your knowledge of other cultures comes from.

Now look at the following advice on how to tackle a short story. Much of it may already be familiar from your work at Key Stage 3 but it is useful to remind yourself before you start reading.

Tackling A Short Story

Although a short story and a novel do have a lot in common, they arc really very different. You will recognise the basics they share:

PLOT   CHARACTER   SETTING AND TIME   THEME

> * A short story, however, usually has:
>   ► a simple plot
>   ► a limited number of characters who are not described in great detail
>   ► one outcome, which is generally surprising and often delivered in the last sentence.

Short stories can be read all in one go – which is in fact the best way to tackle them. Read a story for the first time fairly quickly, to get the outline of it, then read it a second time more thoroughly, and you'll notice much more.

They are often connected in *style* and *language* to poetry, and you should be aware of the effect this has. Linking sections can be missed out and the stories use *metaphors* and *symbols* to put across their *theme* – a theme is what the story is about overall: what its point or message is.

Now let's look at the make-up of the short story.

STRUCTURE – A short story has three parts, which will need to be tackled individually.

1 *The Beginning* – the opening paragraphs are called the *exposition*, because they 'expose', or make clear, what the plot or action is going to be about, and who the main characters are.

2 *The Middle* – this develops the story and provides a life-changing event, generally known as the *complication*. In 'Country Lovers' for example, it is Thebedi's pregnancy.

3 *The Ending* – unlike a novel, in a short story there is only space for one **climax**, or height of interest, though some end with an *anti-climax*, a sudden dropping-away.

CHARACTERS – All of the stories are concerned with people, who come in all shapes and sizes, and with a range of personalities.

TIME AND PLACE – All the stories you will be studying are set in a particular place and period in history, which are essential for understanding the story.

You should remember this equation:

$$\textbf{Time} + \textbf{Place} = \textbf{Culture}$$

When you read the stories you must keep their culture in mind.

NARRATION – It will usually become clear who is telling or *narrating* the story in the first sentence or two. Many writers use an *autobiographical* style, where the narrator is part of the story and refers to himself or herself as 'I'. Some short stories, such as 'Country Lovers' use a type of *fly on the wall* style called *third-person narration*. He or she witnesses events rather than takes part in them.

'Country Lovers'

BY NADINE GORDIMER

Before Reading

Setting

The story is set on a South African farm during the time of Apartheid, a system of government that separated white and black people. A white boy, Paulus, the son of a farm-owner, has a relationship with a black girl, Thebedi, and makes her pregnant. By the time she has the baby, she is the wife of Njambulo, in an arranged marriage.

* Use the library or Internet to find out more about:
   ▶ the 'colour bar' that operated in South Africa before 1994
   ▶ the effects of the Sharpeville Massacre of 1960
   ▶ the Immorality Act that prevented whites and blacks from having a sexual relationship.

* Read the opening paragraph, which tells us that when they were very young, black and white children had no difficulty playing together on equal terms.
   ▶ What does this tell us about natural attitudes to race?
   ▶ Why is this information necessary for the rest of the story?

Exploring the Text

Characters

The main characters are Paulus, Thebedi and her husband Njambulo. The story, written by a white South African author, is told in the third person, in a tone that is cool, unemotional and rather matter-of-fact.

* In pairs, one partner should take the character of Paulus and the other, Thebedi. Write down your responses to the following questions and then discuss how different the two characters are:
   ▶ What is the first description that you form of your character? Make a note of your mental picture of their appearance and personality.
   ▶ In what tone or manner does your character speak? What does he or she talk about, and what does this tell us?
   ▶ What is your character's relationship with the other?

Themes

The story is concerned with the natural feelings of people for each other, in conflict with the race laws.

* In groups, discuss the theme of forbidden love. Thebedi tells the other girls that she has a 'sweetheart'. The word 'love' is never used between them, however.

* What kind of relationship do they have in the early stages? Are they in love?

* Compare and contrast the education and upbringing of Paulus and Njambulo and their attitudes to Thebedi's baby.

* How have the characters and relationships changed as a result of the trial at the end of the story?

SPEAKING & LISTENING

1 What are the circumstances of the baby's death? Write down under 'facts' what you are actually certain about and under 'suspicions' what you imagine might have happened.

2 Use this information to construct the trial scene, with members of the class taking the parts of the judge, the defending and prosecuting counsels, Paulus, Thebedi, Njambulo and other witnesses.

3 Here is a time-chart showing important events related to the characters growing up. You will find this useful for revision.

TIME	EVENT
Paulus and Thebedi are small children	Black and white children play together – they catch a leguan down by the riverbed.
Paulus and Thebedi aged 12	Paulus goes to boarding school. When he returns for Christmas holidays, he and Thebedi secretly exchange presents.
Paulus and Thebedi aged 15	Paulus attends dances with white girls; gives Thebedi the gilt earrings. Head girl has a crush on him. Thebedi occasionally works as a house-servant at his home. During summer holidays, he regularly meets Thebedi by the riverbank. He takes her to his house. Njambulo learning brick-laying skills.
Paulus aged 18; Njambulo aged 19	Paulus is at veterinary college. Njambulo's and Thebedi's parents arrange their marriage. Njambulo builds a hut and marries her. Two months later a baby is born. Paulus returns for holidays. Death of baby. Police examine baby's body.
Paulus aged 19; Njambulo aged 20	The case comes to court. Paulus is found not guilty. Njambulo is commended for looking after the baby.

Discuss the chart. Can you add any events to this chart?

NOTE! Once you have finished reading the other stories, construct your own time-charts, showing how long a period is covered in each story.

WRITING ACTIVITY

Write about the life and character of Thebedi.

Use the following to help you:
- ▶ Consider her lack of choice when it comes to a husband.
- ▶ She does not tell Paulus about her marriage plans, or Njambulo about who the father of her child is.
- ▶ Do we blame her for either example of keeping quiet? What else could she have done?
- ▶ When she gives birth two months after marriage, there is no disgrace amongst her family or people. Comment on the contrasting attitudes of the white and black communities.
- ▶ At the trial she wears the earrings that Paulus had given her several years before. Suggest reasons why.

'Veronica'

BY ADEWALE MAJA-PEARCE

Before Reading

Setting

It is set in an African village in the middle of the last century. There is very little description of this village and none of the city that Okeke moves to. Use your school library or the Internet to find out about the author, Adewale Maja-Pearce, most of whose stories are set in his native Nigeria.

Exploring the Text

Characters

The story is told in the first person by Okeke, the 'I' of the story. One of the drawbacks of this type of narration is that he does not know what is going on in his native village whilst he is in the city. Okeke is intelligent and ambitious, while Veronica, the girl he grew up living next to, is bullied by her father, and grows up passively accepting whatever fate brings her.

As you read the story look out for clues to Okeke's character. Make a chart, listing as many of his characteristics as you can think of and giving supporting evidence.

Two have been started for you:

CHARACTERISTIC	EVIDENCE
He is caring.	He helps Veronica to fetch water and occasionally chops wood.
He's intelligent, hard-working and ambitious.	He wins a scholarship to university and qualifies as a doctor.

✱ Discuss what Okeke means (line 36) when he says he was 'appalled and frightened by her fatalism'.

✱ Look up the word 'fatalism' in a dictionary if you don't feel you understand it. Look for the evidence of her fatalism in the story.

✱ Do you think Okeke should have done more to persuade Veronica to go with him? Write down three arguments he might have used to win her over.

Themes

The story makes a very important point about traditional Nigerian roles for men and women. Opportunities existed for Okeke that did not for Veronica. Whilst he is gaining a scholarship to prepare himself for the outside world, she is being beaten into submission by her father. Whilst he could qualify as a doctor, her lack of education suited her only for the traditional role of cooking for her family, and so on. She has little alternative but to stay at home and wait for a man to come along.

✳ We learn in the opening paragraphs, that Veronica is beaten by her father.
  ▶ What are the reactions of other people, including Okeke, to this?
  ▶ Why was nothing done to stop the beatings?
  ▶ What would you have done?

✳ Veronica turns down a move to the city for a number of reasons. Discuss them under the following headings:
  ▶ her lack of education and qualifications
  ▶ her loyalty to her family
  ▶ her 'fatalism' and general low expectations of life
  ▶ the fact that it is much harder for a woman to leave than a man.

Here is a bar chart showing the relative importance of the events of the story.

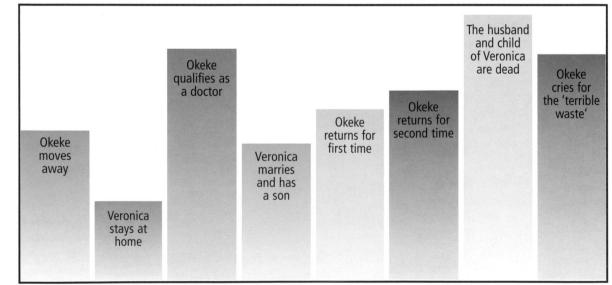

RELATIVE IMPORTANCE →

EVENTS

✳ Discuss the chart. Do you agree with it? Construct your own, finding reasons to change it around. You might, for example, feel that Veronica's marriage is far more important than Okeke's qualification as a doctor.

NOTE! When you have read the other stories, construct bar charts for them, showing the relative importance of characters, events, ideas, or themes.

SPEAKING & LISTENING

In pairs, play the parts of Okeke and Veronica, and act out the scene when he announces that he is leaving (lines 18–48).
He is trying to persuade her to go with him.
She is tempted but hesitant and unconvinced.

WRITING ACTIVITIES

1 Look closely at the episode, in lines 68–105, in which Okeke visits Veronica. It is told through dialogue, and in pairs you should first act it out. It will be interesting to compare the tones different actors adopt and the different stresses they place on words and phrases. Each pair should explain how they attempted to dramatise it.

Now, write about Veronica, using the following questions to help you:
▶ What do we learn from this passage about her life and character?
▶ Why did she stay on, bearing in mind all her brothers and sisters were able to leave?
▶ What is her attitude to her husband?
▶ 'We are managing and God has blessed us with a son.' What does this tell us about her attitude to life?

2 Consider how the relationship between Okeke and Veronica is destroyed by circumstances outside their control.

'The Schoolteacher's Guest'

BY ISABEL ALLENDE

Before Reading

Setting

The story is set some time in the recent past in Agua Santa, a remote village in Chile, which is described as 'an insignificant backwater like so many others on the edge of the jungle' (lines 132–133).

✱ What might life be like in a village of this kind? Think about the significance of its being 'on the edge of the jungle'.

✱ Consider the impact of the opening paragraph.
  ▶ What tone is it written in?
  ▶ How effective is it in making you want to read on?

Exploring the Text

Characters

The main characters are Ines, the schoolteacher, and Riad Halabi, a Turkish shopkeeper who has long been her friend. The story seems to be told in the third person, but an observing, non-participating first person narrator comes out in the last six words of the story.

✱ Look closely at lines 63–75, and then discuss what kind of personality, reputation and authority Ines has.
  What do we learn about the local people from their attitude to her?

✱ Now concentrate on Riad Halabi. Write down a list of all we know about him.
  ▶ What kind of man is he – how would you characterise him?
  ▶ Why does Ines turn to him for help?
  ▶ What would you say is his contribution to the story?

Here is a motive chart showing why the characters acted as they did.

CHARACTER	MOTIVE
Ines's son	To get a free mango.
The 'murderer'	To stop people coming on his land, taking his mangoes.
Ines	To gain revenge for the death of her son.
Riad	To help Ines to escape being caught.
Townspeople	Revenge? Help Ines? Sport? Celebration? Community spirit?

3 Discuss the chart. Can you think of any other possible motives that the townspeople may have had?

NOTE! Make motive charts for some of the other stories, where you think it is appropriate.

Themes

The central theme in the story is revenge, particularly as a bloodsport. Even though the widow's son was killed by accident, the townsfolk agree with her right for revenge, and there is great rejoicing that 'justice' has at last been done.

✳ Consider whether attitudes in Agua Santa towards the 'murderer' might have been different if:
  ▶ He was not an outsider.
  ▶ He had stayed to face a trial.
  ▶ Ines had not been such a respected figure.

✳ Discuss, in pairs, the impact of the two twists in the final six lines, considering:
  ▶ Which is the more surprising – Ines's sudden and unexpected declaration of love for Riad, or the narrator's sudden and unexpected appearance in person to reveal that she had not only witnessed the events but had also been part of the cover-up?
  ▶ Do they form an effective ending to the story?

SPEAKING & LISTENING

In pairs, imagine you are one of the local people telling a friend in another village about these events. What would you say? Use the following to help you:
  ▶ Try to bring out the community's sense of justification.
  ▶ The friend should find it all difficult to understand and ask questions to get the whole picture.
  ▶ Different pairs should choose different characters, e.g. the Doctor, one of the veteran soldiers, Riad, the priest, and so on.

WRITING ACTIVITY

When the men return to Ines's house after getting rid of the body, they eat, drink and 'chatter about the latest cockfights'. What attitudes to revenge are revealed in the story? Use the following to help you:
  ▶ Could only a community that enjoyed blood sports have behaved in this way?
  ▶ How important is the remoteness of Agua Santa?
  ▶ Could you imagine this story taking place today?

'The Gold Cadillac'

BY MILDRED TAYLOR

Before Reading

Setting

This story takes place in the USA, in the year 1950. It begins in Detroit, a northern, industrial city where racism was not such an issue. It moves to Mississippi, a stronghold of racism at the time.

Racial prejudice against Black Americans was strong in the South before the Civil Rights Act of 1964. Do some research on this Act and the events leading up to it, using the Internet or your school library.

✱ In small groups, discuss what prejudice means to you. Do you think it still exists today?

Exploring the Text

Characters

The main characters are 'lois (short for Eloise), a young black girl, and her parents. The story is narrated in the first person by 'lois. Her viewpoint is that of an innocent, questioning youngster who cannot understand why racism exists.

✱ How do you think the story would be different if it wasn't told by 'lois but by:
a) her father?
b) her mother?

✱ Compare the points of view of 'lois's mother and father about the car. Who do you agree with and why?

Themes

The Cadillac, brand new and gold in colour, is a very important symbol in the story. It shows that the black family who owns it is no longer poor and downtrodden, and highlights the main theme of conflict within the story. There are two areas of conflict, one within the family and one within society.

✽ In groups, discuss the theme of conflict within the family, using these questions as a guide:
   ▶ Why is 'lois's mother against the car?
   ▶ Why does 'lois's father want so much to drive to Mississippi in it?
   ▶ What is the reaction of the white southerners to the car and why?
   ▶ After the car has been sold, the family is together again. What does this tell us?
   ▶ How important are family love and self-respect when fighting racial prejudice?

Here is a spider diagram showing the impact of the car on the story.

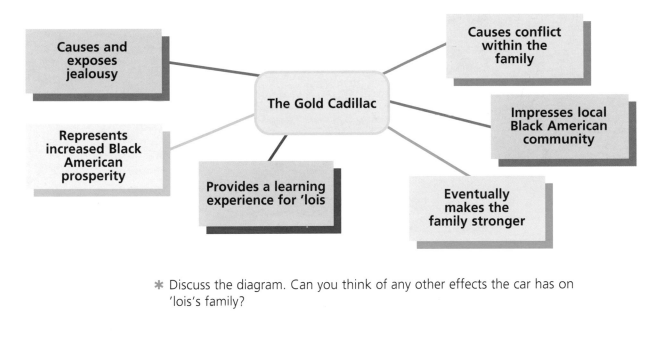

Causes and exposes jealousy

Causes conflict within the family

The Gold Cadillac

Represents increased Black American prosperity

Impresses local Black American community

Provides a learning experience for 'lois

Eventually makes the family stronger

✽ Discuss the diagram. Can you think of any other effects the car has on 'lois's family?

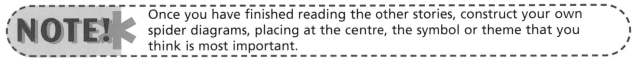

NOTE! Once you have finished reading the other stories, construct your own spider diagrams, placing at the centre, the symbol or theme that you think is most important.

SPEAKING & LISTENING

Read the episode in lines 160–182. In small groups act out the roles of Mr Pondexter, an uncle, the father and the mother, arguing:

▶ whether it is wise to go to Mississippi in the car

▶ whether the women and the children should go on the trip.

It may be useful to arrange the conversation in a playscript first.

WRITING ACTIVITIES

1 'lois says she will never forget her ride to Memphis in the gold Cadillac. Why was it so memorable, and what did she learn about racial prejudice?

Use the following to help you:
▶ What were the conditions like for black people?
▶ How did 'lois feel about what happened to her father?
▶ How did her father react to it?
▶ What were her mother's feelings?
▶ What are your reactions to the episode?

2 From your reading of 'The Gold Cadillac', what have you learned about the nature and effects of racial prejudice?

You may wish to consider:
▶ the effects on family life
▶ the effects on children growing up.

'A Stench of Kerosene'

BY AMRITA PRITAM

Before Reading

Setting

It is set in the mid-twentieth century, in the mountainous and largely Hindu district of Northern India called Jammu and Kashmir. Chamba is a town of some importance; Lakarmandi is a small village close by.

Research and discuss in groups the cultural issue of arranged marriage, giving your opinions on its rights or wrongs – before going on to read the story.

Exploring the Text

Characters

The main characters are Manak and Guleri. Manak's mother is an important force, though scarcely comes in as a character. The story is told in the third person by an omniscient narrator, i.e. one who sees and knows everything about the story.

✳ Read the first 40 lines and then list evidence of the two characters' contrasting points of view in a log like this.

He is dreading the second marriage.	She is excited about going to her parents' home and the fair.

✳ How do you think the story would be different if it was told in the first person by Manak? Write out a paragraph he would have included, showing *his* feelings.

✳ Compare the points of view of Manak and his mother about the second wife. This can be done in the form of a chart, showing arguments and counter-arguments. See the example at the top of page 132.

MANAK	MOTHER
'Guleri may yet have a baby.'	'I have given her seven years to have one.'

Themes

The central theme in the story is the conflict between a man's love for his wife and the obligation to have children. The major cultural issue concerns a man taking a second wife in order to do this. The author tells us that this practice was not unusual in certain parts of India, when the wife was thought unable to fulfil her sacred duty to have a baby. The Hindu Marriage Act of 1955 made it illegal.

✳ What do the following quotations tell us about life for the young wife?
   ▶ 'Guleri was allowed to spend a few days with her parents' (lines 9–10).
   ▶ '. . . the girls looked forward to their annual reunion, talking about their joys and sorrows' (line 11).
   ▶ 'She went about her daily chores – fed the cattle, cooked food for her parents-in-law . . .' (line 18).

✳ Discuss the role played in the story by Manak's mother. Do you think the author wants us to condemn her?

SPEAKING & LISTENING

1 Script and act out the conversation that must have taken place between Manak and his mother about the new wife.
   ▶ He is reluctant.
   ▶ She is determined and feels that it is absolutely necessary.

Both should try to put over their points persuasively.

Plot Graph for 'A Stench of Kerosene'

Here is a plot graph, marking the most important events of the story.

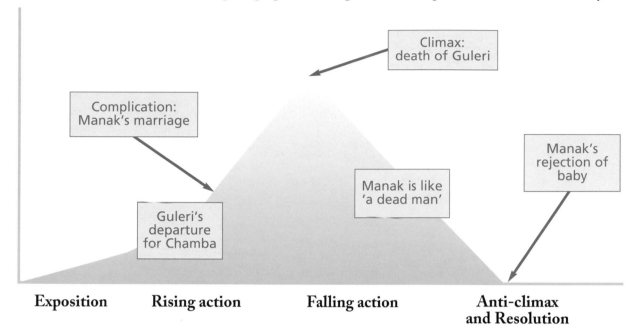

Climax:
death of Guleri

Complication:
Manak's marriage

Manak's
rejection of
baby

Manak is like
'a dead man'

Guleri's
departure
for Chamba

Exposition   **Rising action**   **Falling action**   **Anti-climax
and Resolution**

2 Discuss the graph. Do you agree with this choice of events? What others
would you include, and why?

NOTE! Once you have finished reading the other stories, construct your own plot
graphs, labelling carefully the events in each story that you think are most
important to the plot.

WRITING ACTIVITY

What do you learn about attitudes to love and marriage in this story?

You should consider the following:
▶ the relationship of Manak and Guleri – what evidence is there to suggest that
theirs was a love match?
▶ the views of Manak's mother
▶ Guleri's suicide
▶ Manak's feelings of guilt.

'Vendetta'

BY GUY DE MAUPASSANT

Before Reading

Setting

The story is set in Corsica and Sardinia, in 1880, two islands famous for their blood-feuds. You may have come across the idea of the blood-feud if you studied *Romeo and Juliet* (See Unit 4 of this book).

* Before reading the story debate the question of the blood-feud.
  ▶ Is revenge ever justifiable?
  ▶ Why is it seen in some societies so important to avenge the death of someone from your family?

* After discussion, write down three points you would use to persuade someone not to take out a vendetta against the killer of their son.

Exploring the Text

Characters

The main character is the widow Saverini, although we hear of her son, Nicholas, and his killer Ravolati.

* Write out the widow's diary entries:
  ▶ on the day she swore the vendetta
  ▶ some time while she was training the dog
  ▶ on the night before she set off to Sardinia.

Bring out her thought and feelings, showing how they change with the passage of time.

Here is a ripple diagram, showing how events ripple outwards and the widow's emotions change. (Read it from the centre outwards.)

* Discuss the diagram. What other events would you include in this diagram, and why?

 Once you have finished reading the other stories, construct your own ripple diagrams, showing how events ripple outwards.

Tone

Take it in turns to read the story out loud. The tone is very unemotional and matter-of-fact. What effect does the author achieve by this? Can it be read in any other way? What does the detailed description in the first 40 lines reveal to you about the setting of the story?

Choose five or six descriptive expressions from this section, and say why they are so good at setting the scene and creating the atmosphere.

Themes

This story's central theme is revenge. The mother solemnly swears to revenge her son's death and cannot rest until having achieved it. Does the story seem to you to be in favour of revenge as a form of justice or against it?

SPEAKING & LISTENING

Before going to Sardinia to gain her revenge, the widow goes to 'confession and communion, in an ecstasy of devotion'. In pairs, act out for the class the conversation you imagine took place between the widow and her priest. It may help if some of the conversation is scripted.

Use the following to help you:
- ► Clearly she does not feel that she is about to do something that religion would condemn.
- ► The priest would try to convince her against it.

WRITING ACTIVITIES

1 The method of revenge comes to the widow as 'an inspiration of savage, vindictive ferocity'. Does the story portray revenge as savage and vindictive – and, therefore, to be condemned, or do we sympathise with her?

2 From your reading of 'Vendetta', what have you learned about the nature and power of revenge? You may wish to consider:
- ► the manner of Nicholas's death
- ► the Sardinian setting and culture
- ► the character and age of the widow
- ► some of the language the author uses to describe the act of revenge.

Preparing for the Exams

The questions set for the examination on Different Cultures and Traditions require you to look at the skills the writers use to 'craft' their stories – their language, structure and presentation, and the content of their stories – all the things you've studied throughout the course. You will be asked to write about two stories (at least one of which will be named) and discuss a common theme. This means you need to start thinking about the stories in pairs. You will find this chart really useful when deciding which stories to compare.

STORY/ THEME	CADILLAC	VENDETTA	COUNTRY LOVERS	VERONICA	SCHOOL-TEACHER	KEROSENE
Racism	✓		✓			
Revenge and justice		✓			✓	
Failed relationships			✓	✓		(✓)*
Love torn apart by culture			✓			✓
Threat to family/ community	✓	✓	✓	(✓)*	✓	✓
Can you think of a theme?						

* The brackets indicate that the themes are present but less strongly than in the other stories.

Hint!

You can see from this chart that 'Country Lovers' is a very important story that could be paired with at least three other texts.

See if you can add to this chart, finding other pairings.

EXAM PRACTICE QUESTIONS

Higher Tier

Both 'Vendetta' and 'The School Teacher's Guest' deal with ideas of justice and revenge.

How do you think the writers show the personal and cultural forces that lead to characters taking their revenge? In your response you should refer closely to the texts.

Foundation Tier

The stories 'Country Lovers' and 'The Gold Cadillac' look at young girls learning hard and painful lessons about racism. How are the girls presented in these stories?

You may care to consider:
- ▶ their background, education and family
- ▶ their hopes and beliefs
- ▶ the cruel lesson they learn
- ▶ words and phrases used to describe them and their lives.

4 Shakespeare – *Romeo and Juliet*

Shakespeare's Theatre

Whichever play you have studied, a knowledge of Shakespeare's theatre is essential to understand the time and conditions in which it was produced.

How much do you know? Test yourself to see:
- ▶ What shape was the theatre?
- ▶ How many levels were available to the actors?
- ▶ Where were the audience?
- ▶ What props were used?
- ▶ How were costumes used?
- ▶ What kind of stage sets were used?
- ▶ Who played the women's parts, and why?
- ▶ Why was the *language* so important?

Compare your answers to other people's and see what you left out, if anything.

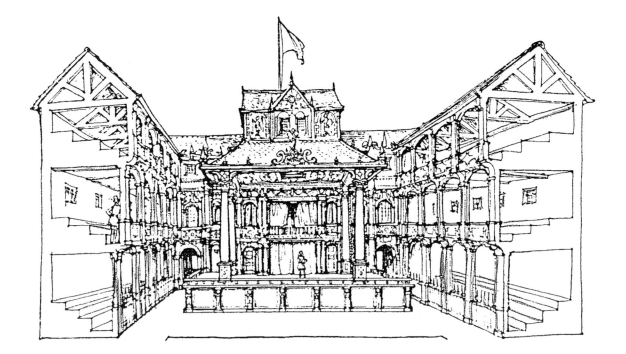

A theatre from Shakespeare's time

Plays in Shakespeare's day ...

These fell largely into three broad groups:

Tragedies:

Tragedies told sad stories in which people often died, or were murdered, for example, in *Hamlet*, *Othello*, and *Romeo and Juliet*. Characters' motives included jealousy, revenge, lust and ambition.

Comedies:

Comedies were often about love and marriage, or misunderstandings, and ended happily, for example, *A Midsummer Night's Dream*, *As You Like It*, and *The Merry Wives of Windsor*.

Histories:

Histories told what happened in the reign of different kings, e.g. *Henry V*, *Richard III*, and *King John*. They combined elements of tragedy *and* comedy.

The Five Act Play ...

This was the basic Elizabethan dramatic structure. It worked like this:

ACT 1: introduced the main characters, the setting, the basic situation, the beginnings of the plot.

ACT 2: developed the plot further and introduced complications or difficulties for the main characters.

ACT 3: introduced yet more complications or problems and furthered the plot; sometimes there were reversals of what the audience expected.

ACT 4: brought about the decisive action or main incident which led to ...

ACT 5: which 'unraveled' all the complications of the plot and showed what happened to all the characters.

Viewed diagrammatically the structure of the Five Act Play would look something like this:

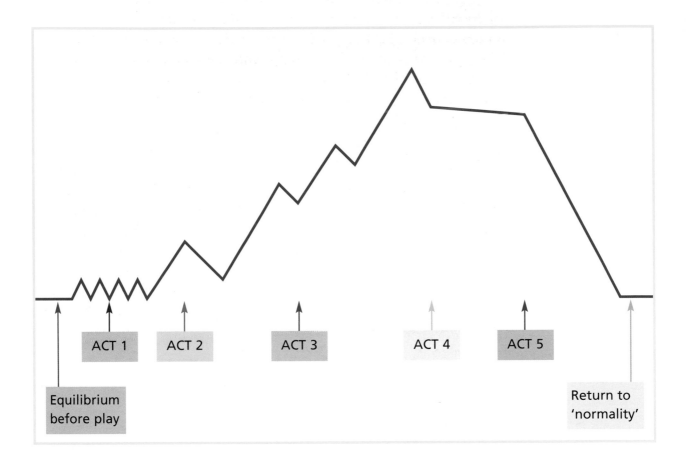

KEY:
Act 1 = inciting incident (what sets 'action' off)
Act 2 = complications (more difficulties)
Act 3 = reversals (unexpected happenings)
Act 4 = climatic action (action which leads to conclusion)
Act 5 = dénouement (conclusion which 'ties up' loose ends of plot).

Background to *Romeo and Juliet*

The play was written in about 1595. Shakespeare took his plots from various sources: the plot for *Romeo and Juliet* was taken from Arthur Brooke's poem 'The Tragicall Historye of Romeus and Iuliet', written in 1562. The play is set in Verona and Mantua, several centuries earlier. English people of Shakespeare's time regarded Italy as an immoral country, famous for illicit sexual affairs and violent crime, and many playwrights set plays there.

Shakespeare depicts medieval Italy as very violent, with duels, street fights, wars, and feuds or mini-wars between opposing families. There was no one to enforce law and order. One man, the Prince of Verona, was in sole charge and could decide the fate of criminals: often death or banishment. Daughters *belonged* to their fathers and wives to their husbands, who could *dispose* of them how they chose. For the wealthy *arranged* marriages were the norm: fathers chose their daughters' husbands from a pool of possible suitors on the basis of wealth, position and family suitability. It was a daughter's duty to obey her father's wishes, whether she liked the suitor or not. *Romantic love was not the basis of marriage.*

Because life expectancy was quite short, it was usual to marry early: Juliet was aged between 13 and 14 when her father arranged for Paris to marry her. Many girls of this age were 'happy mothers made', and Juliet's own mother was a similar age when she had Juliet. It is important to realise how rigid and controlled family life was then compared to now. Women had far less choice in their own destinies; and when Juliet defied these conventions and secretly married not only the man of *her* choice but also the son of *her family's* deadly enemy, the scene was set for tragedy. She was too *modern* to survive in a late medieval society. She wanted more freedom than it allowed her.

Tragedy and Its Causes

What is tragedy? Here is a simple definition:

> **Tragedy** ends badly, comedy ends well.

So far, so good. In real life, if a man falls under a bus and is killed, it is a *tragic accident*. For a play to be a *tragedy* it has to be more than a series of tragic accidents.

Fate has to play a part (e.g. Romeo and Juliet are described as 'star-crossed lovers', as though their fate was 'written' in the stars before they were even born); and *inevitability* (which means that the action was *bound* to happen and no one could stop it).

When fate and inevitability are present, the audience feels:

Pity for the main characters, and
Fear for what is going to happen.

There is also usually some sort of *a great idea* present, such as: perfect love; becoming a King, revenging a real or imagined wrong; an overwhelming ambition, and so on, which turns out disastrously for the main character, leading to a sense of *tragic waste* for what their lives *could* have been.

So, summing up, here is a fuller definition:

> Tragedy is brought about by **fate** and has an **inevitability** about it, and inspires **pity**, **fear** and a sense of **tragic waste** in the audience.

The Prologue and Its Purposes

Remind yourself again of The Prologue:

The Prologue

Two Households, both alike in dignity,
In fair Verona (where we lay our scene),
From ancient grudge break to new mutiny,
Where civil blood makes civil hands unclean.
From forth the fatal loins of these two foes
A pair of star-crossed lovers take their life;
Whose misadventured piteous overthrows
Doth with their death bury their parents' strife.
The fearful passage of their death-marked love,
And the continuance of their parents' rage,
Which but their children's end nought could remove,
Is now the two hours' traffic of our stage;
The which if you with patient ears attend,
What here shall miss, our toil shall strive to mend.   (*Exit*)

SPEAKING & LISTENING

Discuss, in pairs:

▶ What are the purposes of The Prologue?
▶ What is the essential information that it gives the audience? Use: 'There were two families of equal status . . .' to start you off.
▶ What sort of play will the audience expect to see after hearing it?
▶ What idea is introduced by the phrase, 'star-crossed lovers'?
▶ What effect is 'their children's end' going to have on the parents?

To get you thinking . . .

Before you start your coursework essay, here are two 'Speaking and Listening' topics to stimulate your thoughts:

SPEAKING & LISTENING A

1 Is there such a thing as 'love at first sight'?

2 Or is it just strong sexual attraction or infatuation?

3 How much do Romeo and Juliet 'see' of what they are getting themselves into?

4 Were Romeo and Juliet wise or foolish to act as they did?

5 Would you be prepared to deceive or defy your family if they disapproved of your relationship?

SPEAKING & LISTENING B

1 Hot-seat the following characters in turn and question them about what they did or knew at different times in the play: Old Capulet, the Nurse, Friar Lawrence, Paris, Tybalt, the Prince of Verona, Mercutio.

2 Then, as a group, try to put them in rank order of their responsibility for the final outcome of the play.

Your Coursework Essay: *Romeo and Juliet*

It is important to show good knowledge of vital Acts and Scenes that:
- further the plot
- reveal characters' motives, thoughts, actions
- develop main themes, e.g. revenge
- contain vital speeches.

Ten 'Quick Tips' for a Successful Essay

1 PLAN your essay carefully before you start.

2 PICK OUT the quotations you intend to use *and* . . .

3 . . . NOTE where they occur in the play.

4 MAKE your points *simply* and *clearly*.

5 BUILD UP your argument logically, so that it makes complete sense.

6 WRITE clear opening and concluding paragraphs.

7 REFER to the *whole* play, not just a part of it.

8 BUT DWELL more closely on the parts directly relevant to your essay.

9 WEAVE suitable quotations into your own sentences (e.g. "'Even before Romeo arrives at the Capulet ball he has a strange premonition that the 'night's revels' would lead to 'some vile forfeit of untimely death.'")

10 CHECK it over thoroughly for mistakes *before* handing it in!

Essay Option 1:

What makes *Romeo and Juliet* a tragedy, and who or what is responsible for it?

Preparation

* You will need to consider, and make notes on a number of issues, including:
  - What is tragedy?
  - Who does it affect in the play? } include in PARAGRAPH 1

✴ Then, examine the *roles* and *responsibilities* of:

▶ Friar Lawrence   ▶ The Prince of Verona

▶ The Nurse   ▶ Paris

▶ Old Capulet   ▶ Mercutio

▶ The Feud between the Two Families   ▶ Tybalt.

▶ Fate

✴ In conclusion, you will need to sum up who or what you think is most to blame and why.
To get you started, copy out and fill in this chart:

CHARACTER	WHAT THEY DID IN THE PLAY	WHAT YOU THINK THEY SHOULD/SHOULD NOT HAVE DONE	PERCENTAGE (%) OF BLAME
Friar Lawrence			
The Nurse			
Old Capulet			
The Prince of Verona			
Paris			
Mercutio			
Tybalt			
Friar John			

But don't forget *fate* and the *feud*!

In the following pages, we will examine five of the possible 'candidates' for responsibility.

Remember that there are no right answers in an essay like this. In order to get the highest grade, you should consider a number of possible interpretations of the play.

You might use phrases such as the following:
Some might argue that . . .
It could be said that . . .
If you believe that . . ., then you might think that . . .

On your own or in pairs, work your way through the questions for *each* candidate, referring closely to the play as indicated, and making additional notes of your own.

Friar Lawrence

1 Why does he agree to marry Romeo and Juliet? (See beginning of Act 2, Scene 3.)

2 What problems has he not foreseen?

3 What is his attitude to Romeo?

4 What does the Friar mean by, 'These violent delights have violent ends'? (See Act 2, Scene 6.)

5 How does the Friar try to comfort Romeo in the beginning of Act 3, Scene 3? How well does he succeed?

6 Friar Lawrence and Paris in Act 4, Scene 1: how does the Friar behave towards Paris and then towards Juliet when she arrives?

7 Examine Friar Lawrence's 'solution' to Juliet's problems (Act 5, Scene 1, line 68 onwards) *and* his plans to get her away to Mantua.

8 What else could or should he have done at this point in the play? Why didn't he?

9 Examine his reactions to Friar John's news in the beginning of Act 5, Scene 2.

10 Look at Act 5, Scene 3, when he goes to awaken Juliet and finds Romeo dead. Why does he flee? Is he irresponsible? What should he have done?

11 How far is the Friar to be 'condemned' or 'excused'? (See Act 5, Scene 3, line 227.)

The Nurse

1. The Nurse's name is Angelica. Does it suit her behaviour? Is she really Juliet's 'guardian angel'? Give reasons for your answer.

2. Explain what we know of the Nurse's own life and her service with the Capulet family. (See Act 1, Scene 3.)

3. What is her great desire for Juliet?

4. Why does she agree to be the messenger to Romeo in Act 2, Scene 4?

5. Why does she tease Juliet in Act 2, Scene 5?

6. Whose side does she take after the Tybalt–Romeo fight, and why?

7. Why does she tell Juliet to marry with the County Paris after Romeo's banishment? (See Act 3, Scene 5.)

8. When does she defend Juliet? (See Act 3, Scene 5.)

9. When is she completely fooled by Juliet? (See Act 3, Scene 5.)

10. Should she have behaved differently at any time in the play? If so, when?

Old Capulet

1. Why does he not throw Romeo out at the Capulet Ball? (See Act 1, Scene 5.)

2. What is his attitude to Tybalt on that occasion? What does it tell us about him?

3. On which other occasion is Capulet more bloodthirsty? (See Act 1, Scene 1.)

4. What is his attitude to Juliet's marriage early in Act 1, Scene 2?

5. What makes him change his mind?

6. What does he decide, and why, in Act 3, Scene 4?

7. What does he threaten in Act 3, Scene 5, and what mood is he in?

8. What does he mean by 'An you be mine, I give you to my friend'?

9. What does he mean by line 15 in Act 4, Scene 2? Has his attitude to Juliet changed at all?

10. What does he feel at the end of Act 4, Scene 2, and why?

11. How does he behave in Act 4, Scene 5, when Juliet's false 'death' is discovered?

The Feud

1 What are we told about the feud or long-standing quarrel between the Capulets and Montagues, in The Prologue?

2 In which parts of the play does the feud appear?

3 How are Mercutio and the Prince involved in it?

4 What is Friar Lawrence's attitude to it?

5 Why does Tybalt want revenge on Romeo?

6 How is it resolved in the end?

7 How far is it responsible for the tragedy of Romeo and Juliet?

Fate

Consider how fate affects the following characters, scenes or incidents:

1 the Prologue – 'star-crossed lovers'

2 Romeo at the end of Act 1, Scene 5

3 'What must be shall be' (Juliet to Paris, in Act 4, Scene 1)

4 the Capulet Ball in Act 1, Scene 5

5 Friar Lawrence

6 the Tybalt–Mercutio, Tybalt–Romeo fights in Act 3, Scene 1?

7 Juliet's comments in line 60 of Act 3, Scene 5

8 Balthasar seeing Juliet taken to the Capulet vault at the end of Act 4

9 the fact that Friar John's letters did not reach Romeo – delayed by an 'infectious pestilence' in the inn where he stayed

10 At the tomb:
  ▶ Romeo's suicide
  ▶ Juliet's suicide
  ▶ Paris's death
  ▶ Friar Lawrence's escape.

Now you have done all the preparation, you should be ready to start the first draft of your essay.

When your first draft is complete, check it over for mistakes, e.g. punctuation, spelling, paragraphing.

See that it makes complete sense. Put in anything you have left out. Make sure your arguments are clear.

THEN:

Do your second draft. Check it again, as above. If you are happy with it, hand it in!

Other Essay Options:

1 Compare the presentation of **either** Romeo **or** Juliet in a stage or film version you have seen with your own view of the character formed from reading the play.

2 What part does accident and coincidence play in *Romeo and Juliet*?

3 Examine the role of dreams, omens and fate in *Romeo and Juliet*.

4 Explore the contrast between youth and age in *Romeo and Juliet*. Do the generations have anything to teach each other?

5 What impression is given of women's lives in *Romeo and Juliet*? (You should write about Lady Capulet, Juliet, the Nurse and Lady Montague).

Whichever essay you choose, use a similar preparation process to the one outlined for Essay Option 1.

Be prepared to spend time and effort on it and you will succeed.

5 Media

The Specifications

If you are following **Edexcel Specification B**, you will undertake a piece of extended coursework looking at various aspects of Media. This coursework will be worth 5% of the total marks.

Assessment Objectives

The examiners will be expecting you to distinguish between fact and opinion and assess how information is presented. You will be expected to follow an argument, spotting implications and inconsistencies. You will be further required to understand and assess how writers use language, layout and design to achieve their effects and comment on ways language varies and changes.

If, on the other hand, you are studying **Edexcel Specification A** you will be examined on texts you have not seen before in Section A of the 2 hour written examination: Paper 3F or 5H. Your answer will be worth 10% of the total marks.

Assessment Objectives

In addition to the objectives outlined above, the examiners will be expecting you to demonstrate the ability to read with insight and engagement, making appropriate references to texts and developing and sustaining interpretations of them.
You are further required to select material appropriate to your purpose from different sources, and make cross-references.

What *media* means

What does the word *media* actually mean?

Sometimes the term *mass media* is used to describe popular forms of entertainment, such as pop music. *Media* is a plural word meaning a number of different things, such as newspapers, magazines, film, television, radio and the Internet. Their aim is to communicate with as wide an audience as possible.

In this unit you are going to study the way in which information is presented in:
- ▶ newspaper articles
- ▶ magazine articles
- ▶ promotional leaflets.

There will be helpful examination practice questions and coursework questions, where appropriate, following each area. There is also an extra section giving ideas for coursework at the end of the unit (pages 187–190).

In particular you will consider the use of:
- ▶ headlines
- ▶ photographs
- ▶ captions, layout and design
- ▶ language
- ▶ fact and opinion
- ▶ content.

Newspapers

'My God, it's like New York all over again'

LOADED-ON-SEA

Newspapers are the oldest method of *mass* communication and have been in existence for hundreds of years. They aim to:
- ▶ convey information
- ▶ give opinions
- ▶ entertain.

There are two main types of newspapers:
- ▶ the broadsheet
- ▶ the tabloid.

The broadsheets are so-called because the sheets of paper are big and broad, the text is long and uses quite sophisticated vocabulary. The broadsheets tend to concentrate on politics and factual articles, such as medical developments or space travel. They do not usually include much hot gossip. The main broadsheets are *The Times*, *The Daily Telegraph*, *The Guardian* and *The Independent*.

A tabloid newspaper is smaller than a broadsheet and distinguished by huge headlines, many photographs and illustrations and comparatively little text. The stories are written in short paragraphs with short sentences, using simple vocabulary. The style, however, is far from simple, depending on puns and figurative language to convey information in a punchy, entertaining way. They tend to include scandal, 'pin-ups' and gossip about popular figures such as pop stars or footballers. The main tabloids are *The Mirror*, *The Sun*, the *Daily Sport* and the *News of the World*. Tabloid newspapers have a much larger readership than broadsheet papers.

Then there are some *hybrid* or combination newspapers, so-called because they use some of the language of the broadsheets and have a wider range of subject matter than the tabloids. However, they are presented in the tabloid layout. *The Daily Mail* and the *Daily Express* are hybrid newspapers.

Headlines

Headlines are used to catch the reader's attention. In newspaper offices, headlines are often decided after the reporter has written up a story, although they are often the first thing that the public sees.

✳ Therefore, in order to be effective, they need to be:
  ▶ brief
  ▶ eye-catching
  ▶ possibly sensational.

✳ Headline writers try to follow the rules given below:
  ▶ A really good headline uses only two or three words.
  ▶ A headline tells the most important point in the story.
  ▶ A headline uses actual names and figures where possible.
  ▶ A headline expresses a complete thought. The subject and a verb are preferable – but one or other can be left out if the meaning is still clear.
  ▶ A headline uses verbs where possible to add immediacy and impact.
  ▶ A headline leaves out all unnecessary words.
  ▶ A headline does not have a punctuation mark at the end.

Headline **a)** makes a different impact from headline **b):**

a)
THE SUPER SARNIE

b)
Indestructible Sandwiches

Yet both were headlines used in different newspapers to tell the same story about a new, long-lasting sandwich made for the armed forces.

WRITING ACTIVITY

In pairs, discuss and make brief notes in response to the following questions.

1 What difference does the size of the font make?

2 Does it make a difference if the headline is written in capital letters?

3 Does it make a difference if the headline is written in bold type?

4 Why does the spacing between the letters in headline **a)** attract attention?

5 What difference does the use of the word 'sarnie' make? Does the fact that it is in colloquial (spoken) language make it sound more user-friendly?

6 Does it make a difference if the headlines are made up of short, one-syllable words? Are they easier to read and understand?

7 Which account would you rather read, and why?

8 Which sandwich would you rather eat?

WRITING ACTIVITY

Look at the headlines below:

1 Cat thrown 100ft from cliff recovers

2 BAGPUSS SAVED
Holdall cat hurled 100ft off cliff edge

✳ Which of the two headlines would make you read on?

Copy out and complete the table below and on page 157, filling in your responses to the questions for both headlines. Then answer the questions below.

	HEADLINE 1	HEADLINE 2
Is the font size – small or large?		
Is the type of print used – lower case or capital letters?		
Is the text in bold type?		
Does the spacing change?		

	HEADLINE 1	HEADLINE 2
Does the language used attract attention, if so, how?		
Do the headlines use active verbs? What does this add?		
Which headline do you prefer? Complete an entry for both, giving your reasons.		

* What is the difference between 'thrown' and 'hurled'?

* Which sounds more forceful?

* What does the word 'edge' add to the meaning, rather than just 'over the cliff'?

Every picture tells a story

Photographs play a very important part in many articles. We see the photograph before we read the story – and the activity it shows will, along with the headline, help us decide whether or not to read on.

Look carefully at the montage of photographs illustrating the article entitled 'Red Card for Bully Dads who tell Kids to Cheat', from *The Daily Express* (a montage is where other photographs are superimposed on the main picture).

* The montage is set directly opposite the tall headlines, taking up an equal amount of space.

* All the photographs are rectangles.

* The main picture is in vivid colour, while the two small photographs of the football stars show only their heads, and they are, therefore, without noticeable colour.

* This visual contrast helps the photographs to stand out.

* The two men in the smaller photographs are unsmiling and protective. The fact that they look like statues adds an air of nobility.

* The main picture shows lots of activity with the children playing a game of football. The area is pleasantly green, and there are older men looking on.

* Above the photographs and the main headline is a caption. It stands out in white against a black background. This tells the reader that 'football stars' are involved.

* In between the two small photographs of the men is another sub-headline that begins: 'STARRING ROLE' – emphasising their position as football stars. It shows how important their presence is in this campaign.

Red card for bully dads who tell kids to cheat

STARRING ROLE: Rio Ferdinand, left, and Ashley Cole appear in the new FA video which aims to get dads to behave as well as these on the touchline

By **Adrian Lee**

FOOTBALL chiefs are to clamp down on bullying dads whose touchline antics are driving young players out of the game.

They decided to act after it emerged that six- and seven-year-old boys were being encouraged to dive for penalties and foul opposing players.

The Football Association, which has recruited Premiership stars Rio Ferdinand and Ashley Cole to star in a video highlighting the problem, fears the over-zealous fathers are harming grassroots development of the national sport.

Touchline abuse screamed during games is also blamed for a shortage of volunteer referees at junior level and has frequently erupted into violence.

In the latest incident, a father supporting his son's under-15 side bit off the ear of the opposing manager in a punch-up on the touchline.

Peter Tucker, 49, who lost his temper after the team lost 6–2 in East Sussex, was jailed for three years.

County officials have reported numerous cases of children leaving pitches in tears, refusing to play again.

The 10-minute video, called the FA Soccer Parent, will be sent to junior clubs throughout England as part of a drive to improve standards of behaviour.

'We are trying to get across the message that at that age it is not win at all costs,' said Alex Stone, the FA's spokesman for the national game.

'It is only a minority but unfortunately they spoil the game for others. There is so much money in the game now that some fathers see their kids as a meal ticket for the future – they are desperate for them to become the next David Beckham or Michael Owen.

'There are some fathers who stand on the touchline screaming at the kids to hack down an opponent.'

The video features an angry father, played by FA official Les Howie, ranting and raving at young players during a junior match.

'It is tongue in cheek,' said Mr Stone. 'But it makes

an important point that while there is nothing wrong with wanting to win, young kids should be enjoying themselves when they play football, not put under pressure to cheat.'

The game's European and world governing bodies, UEFA and FIFA, are so impressed that they are considering using the video in other countries.

The campaign is part of a £32million scheme to develop the game's grassroots. Money is being provided to train primary school teachers how to get the best from young players and for a national audit of facilities, such as changing rooms and synthetic pitches.

Football chiefs believe there are so many other

sports competing for children's attention, plus the emergence of a 'couch-potato generation' that they must offer good incentives for youngsters to play the sport.

A mini-soccer programme has been introduced, which ensures that children do not play competitive full-scale matches until they are 11 years old.

For younger players, the emphasis is now on developing skills on smaller pitches and there are no leagues so that winning does not become all-important.

The scheme recognises that development of the game at grassroots level has been neglected over the years, with playing fields lost to developers and facilities becoming run down.

● From today, parents who are involved with grassroots football can now go online to learn good practice at www.thefa.com

'It's not win at all costs – some fathers scream at sons to hack down opponents'

WRITING ACTIVITY

In pairs, discuss and make brief notes in response to the following questions about the newspaper article on page 158.

Photographs

1 What ages are the boys in the main picture?

2 What are they doing?

3 Where are they playing? Do you think it is in a town or in the country?

4 What effect do the photographs of the football stars give? Do they look as if they care? Are they smiling?

5 Do they look people whom boys would look up to? Can you describe why?

6 Looking at the montage, how does the arrangement and size of the photographs of Rio Ferdinand and Ashley Cole make them stand out?

Headlines

1 Do we normally think of 'dads' as bullies?

2 Does it make a difference that the familiar word, 'dad' is used, not 'father'?

3 What is it about this headline that is so shocking?

4 What other words tell us that the fathers are behaving badly?

5 How does this help to gain the reader's attention?

6 The caption at the top of the article says 'Exclusive' – what does this tell us?

7 What is the effect of football stars joining the campaign to stop 'touchline pests'?

Would you want to read this article? Give your reasons why or why not.

That's Entertainment

Study the article from the *Daily Mirror* on page 162. It is a very good example of the way in which a tabloid newspaper covers entertainment news.

WRITING ACTIVITY

Using what you have learned about design, layout, photographs and headlines, make brief notes in response to the questions below.

Photographs

1 Describe the amount of photograph as compared with text in this article.

2 Describe the position of the photographs on the page – why do you think that the smaller photograph is not straight?

3 Why is the main photograph given so much space?

4 What 'draws the eye' in the smaller photograph?

5 If you were to look at the main photograph only, would it catch your attention?

6 Describe the clothing that Andrew Lloyd Webber is wearing.

Headlines

1 Describe the main headline in detail referring to the typeface, colour, and the words used.

2 What do the last three letters in the headline refer to?

3 Which did you notice first: the visual aspect of the text or the meaning of the words?

4 Is the fact that the headline is a *play* on Andrew Lloyd Webber's name effective?

5 The caption under the smaller photograph has the first three words in capitals. Why do you think this is so?

6 The sub-headline 'ANDREW'S DAISY DRAG' refers to:
   a) ANDREW: it is a pun on his name, Andrew Lloyd Webber – this is known as a 'play on words'
   b) DAISY: this refers to the name of the play *Daisy Pulls it Off*
   c) DRAG: the fact that he was dressed in drag, as a woman. (It shows use of colloquial language.)

7 What does the caption underneath, 'EXCLUSIVE' tell us? How is this fact emphasised visually?

Content

1 Now read the article carefully. What is its purpose?

2 How do you think it came to be written? Did the *Daily Mirror* contact the producers of the play or vice versa?

EXAM PRACTICE ESSAY

Do you think this article is effective in advertising the play?
Describe what you found interesting or amusing and how it caught your attention.

Your answer should mention the use of:
   ▶ the use of design and layout (including the headlines)
   ▶ photographs
   ▶ captions
   ▶ language and the content of the article.

You should refer closely to the text of the article to support your answer.

I'm Lloyd Webbher

GIRLS ON TOP: Lloyd Webber as the dowdy headmistress with one of the stars of the show

ANDREW'S DAISY DRAG

By JAMES SCOTT

EXCLUSIVE

THE black-rimmed specs, tweed jacket and Robin Hood-style hat are less than flattering – and even the piano's got better legs.

But it's hardly surprising, really.

For the strangely familiar face behind the typically prim, schoolma'am image belongs to musical genius Andrew Lloyd Webber.

The 54-year-old tycoon dressed as stuffy headmistress Beryl Waddle-Browne to promote the new version of his hit play Daisy Pulls It Off.

The schooldays comedy first opened in 1983 to rave reviews and was a sell-out for three years. Now, 16 years later, Lord Webber is bringing it back to the West End.

He said: 'It's a wonderful bit of fun. The cast are pretty much straight out of stage school. But they are fantastic – young, enthusiastic and immensely talented.' The 1920s spoof by Denise Deegan follows the adventures of Daisy, played by Hannah Yelland, who wins a scholarship to posh Grangewood College For Young Ladies.

Hannah says: 'It's a marvellous story of friendship and girls sticking together.'

Lord Lloyd Webber – whose smash hits include Joseph And His Amazing Technicolor Dreamcoat, Jesus Christ Superstar, Evita and Phantom Of The Opera – is excited by his latest project, which opens tonight at the Lyric Theatre. 'I had great fun producing it first time around and I'm looking forward to being part of it again,' he says.

Just one tip Andrew – lose those unattractive Nora Batty stockings.

j.scott@mirror.co.uk

Reporting the News

All newspapers have a basic style for writing news stories. This is known as the Inverted Pyramid.

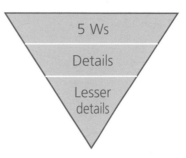

The 5 Ws

The first paragraph includes as many of the 5 Ws as are relevant to the story:
- Who
- Where
- What
- When
- Why (or How).

People often read newspapers in a hurry, so they must be given the most important facts at the beginning of a story. This method is mainly used for writing the news stories that appear on the front cover. Longer articles inside the newspaper, especially when on more specialised subjects, may or may not use the 5 Ws in their opening paragraphs.

News stories are often shortened to fit the page or to make room for a more important story that comes in late. Using this style, it is simple for the editor to shorten the news story by cutting out one or two paragraphs from the end.

Look at the following example:

'Police dog bites off part of boy's ear.'

A boy of 14 needed a six-hour operation to re-attach part of his left ear after it was bitten off by a police dog.	**Who** – a boy of 14. **What** – needed a six-hour operation to re-attach part of his left ear. **Why** – because it was bitten off by a police dog.

WRITING ACTIVITY

In pairs, look at the following opening paragraphs of news stories. Choose six and write out the 5 Ws as shown in the previous example:

1

MOTORISTS are facing blanket speed camera coverage after ten more police forces joined a controversial incentive scheme.

2

Hundreds of people were forced to flee their homes last night as a huge blaze broke out at a chemical plant.

3

QUESTIONS about litter, a play area proposed for a small estate, and the controversial topic about revamping the centre of Uckfield were raised at the annual town meeting on Wednesday.

4

ENGLAND will give David Beckham, their captain and creative catalyst, until the eve of the World Cup finals before even considering replacing him for the summer showpiece following encouraging bulletins on the midfielder's foot injury yesterday.

5

The captain of a school netball team died in a freak accident when she hit her head warming up for a PE lesson.

6

A WIDOW'S 'devious, spiteful and embittered' son stole her husband's collection of vintage cars while she was at a tea dance, a judge heard yesterday.

7

A TINY picture of an eighteenth-century batsman may hide the true South London origins of Marylebone Cricket Club, the home of modern cricket.

8

A POLICE helicopter pilot watched in horror yesterday as a car he was following smashed into railings, killing the 15-year-old driver.

9

ASPIRING Charlie Dimmocks are being encouraged to get their gardening gear on and start digging at the Sandhurst Road allotments in Tunbridge Wells.

Five-hour rescue for stag that leapt 80ft from cliff

By Michael Fleet

A FULL-SCALE rescue operation was launched yesterday after a young deer fell over a cliff and tumbled more than 80ft into the sea.

More than 20 people from the coastguard, the RNLI, the RSPCA and a veterinary practice helped in the five-hour rescue, during which the stag swam more than a quarter of a mile out from the coast at Port Isaac, Cornwall.

The alarm was raised by Jane Byfield, who spotted the deer as it ran along a headland 100 yards from her front window.

She said: 'I have never seen a deer here before and have no idea where it came from. It didn't know where it was going and was clearly distressed.

'At one point it went to the cliff edge and then ran back towards the road but suddenly it turned and headed out. The next thing I saw was the deer in the sea.

'I had called a friend in the local coastguard and then I saw the inshore lifeboat.'

The lifeboatmen shepherded the frightened animal back towards the coast. It came ashore at a secluded cover accessible only by sea or down a sheer, 180ft cliff.

Armed with a tranquiliser gun, Michael King, a vet, was brought to the beach by lifeboat but had trouble sedating the animal.

'At one point the deer ran into a cave and was hiding in the dark,' said Mr King.

After being surrounded by RSPCA officers and lifeboat crew the deer was finally caught and sedated with an injection. It was then put into a harness before being winched up the cliff by the coastguard rescue team.

Ken Richards, the station officer at

The sedated deer, held by a rescue worker, is winched up the cliff

Port Isaac coastguard, said: 'It was a long, and at times difficult operation, but the deer seems to be perfectly all right.'

Mr King said: "It turned out to be a very good swimmer and, despite running over the rocks, it has not received anything worse than a few cuts and scratches. If it had fallen on to the rocks rather than into the water it would have been killed or very badly injured.

'We will take it to woods far away from the coast and release it. It will be a bit stiff for a few days but will soon recover and will hopefully keep well away from the sea.'

Trapped: the young deer swam a quarter of a mile out to sea before returning to shore, where it was sedated and winched 80ft back up the cliff

A Dramatic Event

The article on the previous page is an example of the way in which a broadsheet newspaper (*The Daily Telegraph*) reports a dramatic event. Think about all you have learned about the photographs and headlines.

WRITING ACTIVITY

In pairs, discuss and make brief notes in response to the following questions:

Headlines

1 How do the numbers used in the headline add to the drama of the incident?

2 What do we instantly learn from the headline?

Photographs and their Captions

1 Which photograph is given the most space? How much space is allowed and why do you think this is?

2 Describe the colour in both photographs:
   a) Do you think the contrast is effective?
   b) If so, why?

3 What does the caption under the main photograph tell us? What is the word that is most effective?

4 What do we learn from the smaller photograph about:
   a) the deer?
   b) the rescuers?

5 What does the caption under this picture tell us?

Language

1 Which verbs are used to describe the deer's fall?

2 Which word used to recount the way the lifeboat men guided the deer back to the coast suggests kindness and care?

Content

1 How is the size of the operation described in the first line?

2 In the second paragraph, which organisations are called in? What does this tell us about:
   a) the scale of the rescue?
   b) the importance given to the deer?

3 From whom do we hear the full story of the deer's accident? Why did this person particularly notice the deer?

4 What do we learn about the deer's ability to survive?

First-hand Accounts

This article includes first-hand accounts given by:

a) Jane Byfield, who first reported the incident

b) the vet, who sedated the deer

c) the station officer at Port Issac coastguard, who was involved in the rescue.

These personal statements make the article vivid. Without them we would learn only the facts, but they add personal opinion. For instance, Jane Byfield decided that the deer was 'clearly distressed'. The vet, Mr King, tells us that the deer ran into a cave and was, 'hiding in the dark'. Mr Richards, the coastguard station officer, points out that the deer was 'perfectly all right' but that, as Mr King mentions, if it 'had fallen on to the rocks rather than into the water it would have been killed or very badly injured.'

EXAM PRACTICE ESSAY

Does this article give a clear description of the deer's accident and the way in which it was saved?

Your answer should show the methods used to present the information, and include:

▶ headlines and captions
▶ use of first-hand accounts
▶ photographs and general layout
▶ language and content.

You should refer closely to the text of the article in your answer.

Fact and Opinion

It is a fact that football is the best game in the world.

Do you think it is the best game in the world? Many of you will be certain that it is. However, there are also many people who think other sports are the best in the world; they prefer netball, tennis or swimming. The statement, 'It is a fact that football is the best game in the world' is, therefore, an opinion.

How can you decide what is a fact and what is an opinion?

ACTIVITY

* Decide, in pairs, which of the following sentences are *facts* and which are *opinions*:
  - Jane Austen was a writer.
  - Tony Blair is an excellent Prime Minister.
  - The Wimbledon tennis fortnight takes place in June every year.
  - The earth is round.
  - The earth is flat.
  - Ford cars are the best in the world.

* How did you decide whether the statement was a fact or an opinion? Can you check that you are right?

* Were some statements harder to categorise than others? If so, why might this be?

* Opinions are often written as if they are facts. Why do you think this is done?

A *fact* is something that can be proved to be true, whereas you cannot prove an *opinion* to be the truth. It is what a particular person thinks or feels to be true – but another person may think or feel differently. You need to read carefully, as opinions are used to try to persuade you that someone else's opinion is the truth, as in 'Ford cars are the best in the world'.

The extract on the following page is from an article in *The Sun* that tells the story of a ship on which the wealthy can make their home.

WRITING ACTIVITY

NOW copy out and complete the table that follows, using the text from the article to help you:

QUESTIONS	RESPONSES
Where is The World presently docked?	Tatty junk yard at Greenwich, South East London
What are the facts given about the size of the ship?	
What are the facts given about the costs of buying an apartment on The World?	
How many and what kind of rooms do the apartments have?	
What sports and other activities are catered for?	
What opinions does the newspaper give about The World, its residents or life on it?	
List five colloquial words used in the article and say what you think they add.	
Why did Athena Demartini move to The World?	
What is her opinion of the ship?	
What extra details are we given about Mr and Mrs Demartini?	

LOADED-ON-SEA

A HOLIDAY TOWN THAT SAILS AROUND THE WORLD . . . FOR MULTI-MILLIONAIRES ONLY

WELCOME to the planet's most exclusive address – a luxury liner called The World.

It is a home with a difference because millionaire residents will cruise the seven seas enjoying an ever-changing view. Yesterday the view was a tatty junk yard at Greenwich, South East London. But future locations promise to be more exotic.

If you want to live aboard The World you have to be mega-rich. The cheapest one-bed apartment costs £1.5million. A three-bedroom, three-marble-bathroom penthouse will set you back up to £7million.

The World, built in Norway at a cost of £185million, is on its maiden voyage with residents getting to know their new homes.

It holds 110 apartments and 88 have been snapped up – 11 by rich Brits.

The maiden voyage got off to a stormy start when The World – which at 648ft is as long as an aircraft carrier – set sail in a force nine gale.

On its first voyage, The World will take in 120 ports in 46 countries, ranging from St Petersburg in Russia to Acapulco in Mexico.

It will visit events such as the Cannes film festival and Monaco grand prix before the trip ends in Honolulu next year.

Sparkling

The ship has all the trappings of a five-star hotel and more. All meals and drinks are free and there are 320 staff to attend to residents' needs.

Sparkling in the window of jewellers Graff is a £225,000 diamond necklace if you want to part with some petty cash. The World has a tennis court, two swimming pools, a jogging track, golf range and putting green with real grass. Range balls dissolve harmlessly in the sea.

When not exercising, residents can let their hair down in a nightclub with its own DJ.

New residents include Athena and John Demartini who sold their flat on the 62nd floor of New York's Trump Tower after last year's terrorist attacks.

Athena said: 'When I heard about the ship it seemed like a complete haven. I got so scared after September 11 and I knew I couldn't live in a tower block any more. I adore my apartment. When we moved in, we were greeted by staff who said, 'welcome home' – I love that.'

BY SARA NATHAN

EXAM PRACTICE ESSAY

'What response do you think *The Sun*'s article intends to create in its readers? Does it want them to envy the 'mega-rich' or see the ludicrous side of spending so much money on a floating apartment?

In your answer you should include:

▶ use of headlines
▶ use of photographs
▶ the content of the article
▶ use of language in the first-hand accounts
▶ any other features of layout and design.

Refer closely to the text of the article in your answer.

Emotive language

Newspapers do not simply report the news. That would be very boring and people would soon stop buying newspapers. As readers, we want to be informed but also we want to be entertained, moved and even outraged. How do journalists write in a way that makes us *feel* as well as think?

The following article on page 172 is from the *Daily Mail* and describes the trial of a father who beat up a drug dealer who had supplied his sons with heroin.

WRITING ACTIVITY

✳ With a partner, write a summary of this news story in as few words as possible. Aim for a maximum of 50 words. When you have finished, think about what you were forced to leave out. Is your version as emotive as the original story?

✳ Now go through the article carefully, noting down all the words that convey emotion (for example: 'desperate' in the first sentence).

Father must pay drug dealer who corrupted sons

A MOCKERY OF JUSTICE

By **David Williams**
and **Tom Rawstorne**

FOR six desperate years, loving father Roger Dorrington struggled to free his two sons from the grip of drugs.

Nick and Joseph had been just 14 and 15 when they were introduced to cannabis. That led to Ecstasy, then cocaine and finally heroin.

Their father blamed drug dealer James White for turning his boys into addicts. And what really enraged him was finding that White was corrupting his sons in their own home.

So he banned him from the family's bungalow in a hamlet in the New Forest.

But one day the self-employed builder returned home and caught 24-year-old White in a bedroom cutting up heroin. His anger boiled over and he punched him 15 times in the face and threw him off his property.

To many, Mr Dorrington would be a hero – but then the British legal system intervened.

In a breathtaking example of justice being turned on its head, no prosecution was brought against the drug dealer.

And now a judge has told Mr Dorrington to pay White £250 compensation and sentenced him to 100 hours community service alongside exactly the sort of dealers and criminals he was making a stand against.

Last night Mr Dorrington said he would not pay the money and added: 'I've no regrets about what I did – if anything, I didn't hit him hard enough.'

The court heard he attacked White after realising that he and Nick had been out buying the heroin.

White, of Woodgreen, New Forest, suffered cuts and bruises and complained to

police, who arrested the builder and charged him.

Mr Dorrington, who is divorced from the boys' mother, said his sons were now rebuilding their lives.

Nick, now 20, is living in America, while Joseph, 21, successfully completed a drug treatment order last month.

Joseph said the arrest of his father had 'opened his eyes to the evil of drugs and what he was subjecting his family to.'

The family's MP, Desmond Swayne, said: 'Its shocking. If it was my children, I would garrotted him with his own intestines. I never would have thought I would end up in court having to pay compensation.'

EXAM PRACTICE ESSAY

How does the writer of this article make the reader feel his sense of outrage? Use the information given in the *Daily Mail* to support your ideas.

In your answer you should include comments on:
- ▶ the content of the article
- ▶ the use of headlines
- ▶ the use of photographs
- ▶ the use of language
- ▶ any other features of layout and design
- ▶ your own opinion.

Leaflets

Leaflets are used to give information in a range of situations. Some are promotional leaflets dropping through our letterboxes to sell us double glazing or cleaning products. Others are found in doctors' surgeries, telling us what to do about various ailments. They can also be used to promote an idea, such as suggesting an activity you might like to go to, such as a disco or a car boot sale. They can also tell you about a service, such as gardening or dog-walking.

Nowadays they can also be found on the Internet, in the form of press releases, giving information to the public. So how do they differ from newspaper articles?

Tall Ships Adventures

The Tower and the glory

UPLIFTING: The tall ship with crew on the yard arms at Tower Bridge

MAN THE SAILS: The crew climb the rigging

■ **by NICK LESTER**

TWO Plymouth teenagers got a bird's eye view of Tower Bridge – 118ft up the mast of one of Britain's largest sailing ships.

Passing through one of the country's most spectacular landmarks on the yard arms of the 600-tonne tall ship Stavros S Niarchos was the culmination of a 10-night dream voyage for students Julia Bale and Chris Davies.

Setting out from Ipswich, the journey on board the square-rigged sailing ship took the Plymstock School pupils to the ports of Weymouth and Cherbourg.

During the trip, the youngsters had the opportunity to try their hand at everything from navigating the Channel, manning the yard arms, and even taking the helm of the vessel.

The lucky crew members were selected through Plymstock School for their written submissions on why they wanted to join the trip.

Julia and Chris were from one of 12 schools nation-wide taking part in the voyage.

Plymstock School's headteacher Andrew Parsons said: 'The tall ships' experience complements what we teach in the classroom, giving students real-life situations where they can put their ingenuity and problem-solving to the test and see how they survive.'

Achievement

'In addition to having a fun time, these young people will also come away with a real sense of achievement.'

The giant vessel was named after the wealthy Greek ship owner, the late Stavros S Niarchos, by his daughter Maria Niarchos-Gouaze.

Julia, 17, from Hartley has had some sailing experience on her father's 30ft yacht, but Chris, also 17, had had no experience of life on the ocean waves.

The pair are both in the second year of their A-Levels at Plymstock school, Chris doing computer science, media and physics and Julia taking history, politics and French.

The ship is owned and operated by the Sail Training Association for the personal development of young people through sail training experience on tall ships.

It was specially chartered by the HSBC Education Trust, which works with communities throughout the UK to give teenagers an opportunity to work in a team and learn more about themselves.

fun excitement
challenge teamwork
adventure

A Tall Ship – probably the best environment in the world for providing you with a chance for personal achievement and adventure.

If you're between 16 and 24 you can share in this unique experience. It's different, it's exciting and it's a real challenge!

ready for adventure?

Our impressive Tall Ships set sail from various UK and European ports. Every voyage is special and made unique by the crew! On a typical voyage, our ships will sail up to 1,000 miles, often visiting a European port.

You'll live and work with other young people from different backgrounds and be a vital part of the crew. It's full on and 24 hours a day, but you'll never be bored.

ready for excitement?

The sea is constantly changing and so will your days. It'll be all hands on deck in strong winds and heavy seas, but on

a calm day there'll be time to relax and take in the amazing surroundings.

Brian 19: "This was really the adventure of a lifetime. We were expected to take on all the responsibilities of a normal ship's crew. It was hard work but a lot of fun"

Ed 17: "It was really good fun, we were climbing up masts and doing night look-out duty. We were also able to explore the places where we dropped anchor. All in all it was a great experience and I recommend it to anyone"

The Sail Training Association is dedicated to the personal development of young people through the sail training experience on tall ships

"it's something you'll remember for the rest of your life"

your life on the ocean wave

Your voyage will normally start and end in a European port. All you need to bring with you is a sleeping bag, plenty of warm clothes, pocket money and of course, your passport. We supply everything else – foul weather gear, safety equipment and plentiful food.

"but I've never been sailing before"

• You don't need any sailing experience. Indeed, many have not set foot on a ship at all and the first few hours are spent quite literally 'learning the ropes' and getting to know each other.

• Everyone takes a part in the running of the ship – but don't worry, professional permanent and volunteer crew are there to guide and help you.

• In order to sail the ship 24 hours a day, the voyage crew (that's you!) is divided into three Watches each led by an experienced Watch Leader.

• You will join one of these Watch teams, you will learn to handle the sails and ropes, keep a proper lookout, take the helm, help in the galley, assist the Bosun with repairs and paintwork and generally participate in all the activities of a large sailing ship.

• Remember, a voyage is not a holiday in the usual sense of the word. It's certainly a break from your normal world, but you won't be pampered, cosseted or waited on.

• You'll be working in a team and sometimes tough work at that. But as you step ashore at the end of your adventure we can promise you'll have had an experience that will not only have been incredible fun, but that may well change your whole life and those around you.

Stuart 17: "It's not all work. When you're off watch you have time to take in the splendour of a tall ship at sea and chat to new found friends"

excitement aloft

Going aloft is a really exciting experience and one you'll never forget. You have to wear a safety harness at all times when you are on watch and although no-one is forced to go aloft, most people do. When you are up there you will be setting (letting loose) or handing (folding away) the square sails that make our ships so easy to recognise.

below decks

Accommodation is comfortable and welcoming. You'll sleep in 8 berth cabins. Hot showers are always available.

experienced hands show you the ropes

A Tall Ship adventure is one not to be missed and everyone is encouraged to get involved. Our professional permanent and volunteer crew will always be on hand to give you expert tuition and guidance. Our ships have an excellent safety record. The Maritime and Coastguard Agency safety regulations are strictly observed and more than supplemented by our own codes of practice. We can also give you instruction for the RYA Competent Crew certificate if time and the weather permits.

Find out more by visiting our web site at

www.sta.org.uk

WRITING ACTIVITY

Read the article 'The Tower and the Glory' from the *Plymouth Evening Herald*, and the Sail Training Association leaflet promoting the Tall Ships Adventure, then copy out and complete the following chart, filling both columns where appropriate.

	THE LEAFLET	THE ARTICLE
Does it give a personal account of an experience?		
Does it give details of the general experience?		
What does it tell you that you would need to take with you on a voyage?		
How long is a typical voyage?		
Is it necessary to have sailing experience to take part?		
How many hours would you be expected to be 'on Watch' each day?		
What would you learn to do?		
What first-hand information is given?		

EXAM PRACTICE ESSAY

Using the information in your completed chart, compare the article with the leaflet. Which in your view is more effective?

In your answer you should consider the similarities and differences between the two texts, in their:
▶ use of headlines
▶ use of photographs
▶ general layout
▶ content
▶ use of language – first-hand accounts.

Include your own responses to the article and the leaflet.

Comparing Leaflets

Now look at the four leaflets on this and the following pages. They may be assessed in the same way as newspapers for:

▶ their layout and design (is it attractive and easy to read?)
▶ headlines and captions
▶ photographs and diagrams
▶ use and tone of language (is it right for the subject?).

Leaflet A

Your eye condition

Understanding retinal detachment
Royal College of Ophthalmologists

What is the retina?

Imagine that your eye is like a camera, and the retina is the film. The retina is a fine sheet of nerve tissue lining the inside of the eye (see diagram). Rays of light enter the eye and are focused on the retina by the lens. The retina produces a picture which is sent along the optic nerve for the brain to interpret. It's rather like the film in the camera being developed so that pictures can be produced.

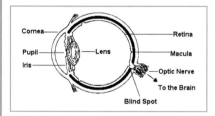

What is retinal detachment?

Usually the retina is attached to the inner surface of the eye. If there is a tear or hole in the retina then fluid can get underneath it. This weakens the attachment so that the retina becomes detached – rather like wallpaper peeling off a damp wall.

When this happens the retina cannot compose a clear picture from the incoming rays and your vision becomes blurred and dim.

Who is more likely to get it?

Detachment of the retina happens more to middle-aged, short-sighted people. It is quite uncommon however and only about one person in ten thousand is affected.

Very rarely, younger people can have a weakness of the retina.

What are the symptoms?

The most common symptom is a shadow spreading across the vision of one eye. You may also experience bright flashes of light and/or showers of dark spots called floaters. These symptoms are never painful.

Many people experience flashes or floaters and these are not necessarily cause for alarm. However, if they are severe and seem to be getting worse, and/or you are losing vision then you should see a doctor urgently. Prompt treatment can often minimise the damage to your eye.

Leaflet B*

DYNAMIC TIGER FREESTYLE KICKBOXING

NOW ENROLLING

MONDAYS
At Broadoak Village Hall
Heathfield
East Sussex
Junior class
7.30 - 8.30
Senior Class
8.30 - 10.00

TUESDAYS
At Uplands Sports Centre
Lower Highstreet
Wadhurst
East Sussex
Senior class
8.30 - 10.00

THURSDAYS
At Uplands Sports Centre
Lower Highstreet
Wadhurst
East Sussex
Junior class
7.00 - 8.00
Senior Class
8.00 - 9.30

Other venues in
West Sussex
East Sussex
Hampshire
& Surrey
- Please ring
for details

Dynamic tiger freestyle kickboxing is a modern day martial arts system with a no nonsense, practical approach to self-defence. Through out our DTFK training programs the student learns a balanced combination of Thai Kickboxing, Jujitsu, Judo, Aikido, and Vale Tudo (Brazilian Ground Fighting). This results in a devastating style which leaves you ready for anything

Head Instructor Jeremy Fitt has had extensive experiance in many martial art forms and has been an instructor with DTFK for over 4 years since he was hand picked and trained by Sensei Damon Kentell - Chief Instructor of Dynamic Tiger Freestyle Kickboxing

We welcome you to train with us in our unique system

UNLIMITED lessons per month
FREE uniform
FREE licence
FREE insurance
FREE gradings
including certificates and sashes

For one monthly payment plan

"Join the fastest growing martial arts system in the south"

IMPROVE:
Co-ordination
Confidence
Awareness
Flexibility
Stamina
Balance
Fitness

LEARN:
Thai Kickboxing
Valetudo
Jujitsu
Aikido
Judo

Plus 1 FREE introductory lesson

* Please note that some of the information in Leaflet B has been updated. For more information, please contact Jeremy Fitt on 01825 732386.

Leaflet C

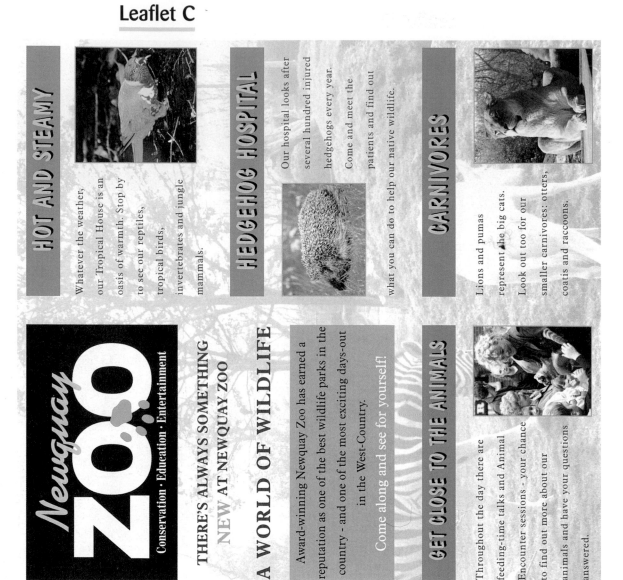

HOT AND STEAMY

Whatever the weather, our Tropical House is an oasis of warmth. Stop by to see our reptiles, tropical birds, invertebrates and jungle mammals.

HEDGEHOG HOSPITAL

Our hospital looks after several hundred injured hedgehogs every year. Come and meet the patients and find out what you can do to help our native wildlife.

CARNIVORES

Lions and pumas represent the big cats. Look out too for our smaller carnivores: otters, coatis and raccoons.

Newquay ZOO

Conservation · Education · Entertainment

THERE'S ALWAYS SOMETHING NEW AT NEWQUAY ZOO

A WORLD OF WILDLIFE

Award-winning Newquay Zoo has earned a reputation as one of the best wildlife parks in the country - and one of the most exciting days-out in the West-Country.

Come along and see for yourself!

GET CLOSE TO THE ANIMALS

Throughout the day there are feeding-time talks and Animal Encounter sessions - your chance to find out more about our animals and have your questions answered.

HEY HEY WE'RE THE MONKEYS

Newquay Zoo's collection of primates is one of the best in the country. See them on their island homes, along the Monkey Walk, or in the Tropical House. Our thriving family of Sulawesi macaques can be found in their award-winning enclosure.

RUNNING FREE

As you walk around the zoo, look out for our free-ranging animals. There are lots of birds, mara from South America and a family of cotton-top tamarins - small monkeys from Colombia.

MEET THE MEERKATS

Visit the award-winning African Plains enclosure, which our large family of meerkats share with antelope, zebra and porcupines.

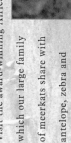

Leaflet D

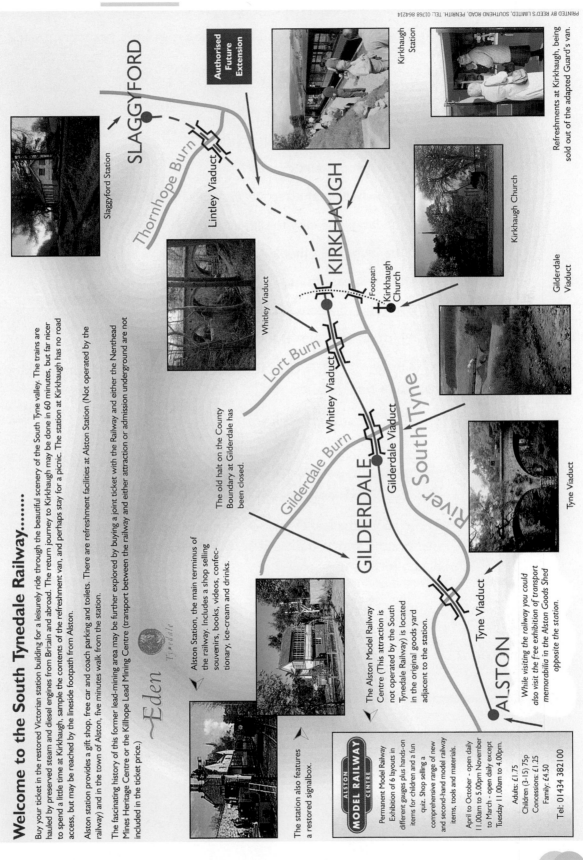

Welcome to the South Tynedale Railway.......

Buy your ticket in the restored Victorian station building for a leisurely ride through the beautiful scenery of the South Tyne valley. The trains are hauled by preserved steam and diesel engines from Britain and abroad. The return journey to Kirkhaugh may be done in 60 minutes, but far nicer to spend a little time at Kirkhaugh, sample the contents of the refreshment van, and perhaps stay for a picnic. The station at Kirkhaugh has no road access, but may be reached by the lineside footpath from Alston.

Alston station provides a gift shop, free car and coach parking and toilets. There are refreshment facilities at Alston Station (Not operated by the railway) and in the town of Alston, five minutes walk from the station.

The fascinating history of this former lead-mining area may be further explored by buying a joint ticket with the Railway and either the Nenthead Mines Heritage Centre or the Killhope Lead Mining Centre (transport between the railway and either attraction or admission underground are not included in the ticket price.)

SLAGGYFORD

Slaggyford Station

Authorised Future Extension

Thornhope Burn

Lintley Viaduct

Kirkhaugh Station

Refreshments at Kirkhaugh, being sold out of the adapted Guard's van.

KIRKHAUGH

Footpath

Kirkhaugh Church

Kirkhaugh Church

Whitley Viaduct

Gilderdale Viaduct

Lort Burn

Alston Station, the main terminus of the railway. Includes a shop selling souvenirs, books, videos, confectionary, ice-cream and drinks.

The old halt on the County Boundary at Gilderdale has been closed.

Whitley Viaduct

Gilderdale Burn

GILDERDALE

Gilderdale Viaduct

River South Tyne

Tyne Viaduct

Eden
Tynedale

The Alston Model Railway Centre (This attraction is not operated by the South Tynedale Railway) is located in the original goods yard adjacent to the station.

Tyne Viaduct

ALSTON

While visiting the railway you could also visit the free exhibition of transport memorabilia in the Alston Goods Shed opposite the station.

The station also features a restored signalbox.

ALSTON MODEL RAILWAY CENTRE

Permanent Model Railway Exhibition of 6 layouts in different gauges plus hands-on items for children and a fun quiz. Shop selling a comprehensive range of new and second-hand model railway items, tools and materials.

April to October - open daily 11.00am to 5.00pm November to March - open daily except Tuesday 11.00am to 4.00pm.

Adults: £1.75
Children (3-15) 75p
Concessions: £1.25
Family: £4.50

Tel: 01434 382100

ACTIVITY

Look first at Leaflets A and B which do not have photographs and make notes on each of them:

1 What is the leaflet about?

2 Is it trying to sell you something?

3 Is it giving you useful information?

4 Which layout looks clearest?

5 Are the headlines effective, easy to see and understand?

6 Is the language easy to understand?

7 Is the language suitable to the subject?

8 Is the text easy to read?

9 Which do you think is the best leaflet, and why?

10 Which do you think is the worst leaflet, and why?

Now look at Leaflets C and D which have photographs and, asking the same questions, make notes on them.

Discuss your answers with a partner.

EXAM PRACTICE ESSAY

Write about the leaflet you found most interesting and appealing, mentioning why you liked it best. Support your comments with suitable detail, including:

▶ the use of headlines
▶ the use of photographs
▶ the purpose of the leaflet
▶ is the language used:
   a) suitable to the subject?
   b) a first-person account?

▶ Is the leaflet mainly based on fact or does it give opinions?
▶ any other features of layout and design
▶ your own opinion.

Refer closely to the texts to support your answers.

Magazines

Magazines are less topical than newspapers, where there is a new or 'news' story every day. They are published weekly, monthly or even yearly, so their articles are:

- more general
- often about the past or future, not just the present
- about people living or dead
- about subjects (e.g. science, gardening or archaeology)
- designed to be read over a longer period.

Their *shelf life* is often months long, then they linger on in doctors' and dentists' waiting rooms. An article about art forgers, English people living in France, or mountaineering in Scotland can have an almost permanent interest-value.

ACTIVITY

What makes a *good* magazine article? How important are the following?

- language
- layout
- photographs and illustrations
- title
- length.

We have already established that its audience and purpose is different from a newspaper article. This chart shows the differences:

NEWSPAPER ARTICLE	MAGAZINE ARTICLE
short, zappy headline for instant impact	longer title
news items in inverted pyramid style	often much longer, going into more detail and depth
photographs	photographs and illustrations
short sentences and paragraphs	longer sentences using more adjectives, and longer paragraphs

WRITING ACTIVITY

✳ Discuss, in pairs, how the news item, news report and magazine article about the missing teenagers use the following:
  ▶ the 5 Ws
  ▶ the inverted pyramid style
  ▶ reporting facts only
  ▶ fact and opinion
  ▶ use of the first person and its effects.

✳ Now answer these questions concerning the magazine article:
  ▶ Which five topics are covered in the five paragraphs?
  ▶ How do the words used differ from those used in the news item and news report? Pick out some examples of these differences.
  ▶ How do the sentences and paragraphs differ? Again pick out some examples.

News Item:

Missing teenager: A 13-year-old girl, Linda Dawson, of Harrogate, Yorkshire, was reported missing by her parents after she did not return home from school yesterday. The police are making enquiries.

News Report:

Following her disappearance yesterday, the police are making enquiries about missing schoolgirl, Linda Dawson. They have been at her school today, taking statements from her friends. Linda had gone to the cinema with two other girls to see a Hugh Grant film. They left the cinema about 9pm and Linda was last seen by them leaving there. She had a half-mile walk to get to her home.

The police have set up an inquiry van outside the cinema and are asking passers-by if they saw Linda. She can be seen on the CCTV cameras setting off down the High Street, but then she turned left into a quieter road, and has not been seen again.

Her parents, Tom and Sally Dawson, are making a TV appearance tonight, in order to try to 'jog people's memories' about the incident. They are distraught – Linda, 17, is due to take her GCSEs this year and has been working hard.

Magazine Article:

Home *and* Away ● ● ●

Every year, about 20,000 people – many of them teenagers – just 'disappear'; as completely as if abducted by aliens and taken to another planet. Their real fate, though not so dramatic, can be equally devastating to those left behind, especially the anxious/guilty/distraught parents. They wait by the phone, give descriptions to the police, even make impassioned pleas on TV for their children's 'safe return' . . . usually to no avail. The missing become statistics, names on files at the Salvation Army, the Social Services, or on police computers.

They creep out in the night with a few belongings, some savings, sandwiches, or spare shoes; sometimes they leave a note, or confide in a friend and swear them to secrecy. Sometimes it follows a quarrel, violence, or abuse; they may be pregnant, or on drugs and tell nobody. If they live in the provinces, their usual destination is London . . . you can get lost there, and beg, or steal, hang out on the streets, somehow survive. There are plenty of jobs, once you get yourself a place . . . there are plenty of dangers, too.

Girls may run away with their 'boyfriends', others abscond from 'care', foster-parents or youth custody. The 'boyfriends' may turn out to be pimps, persuading, or threatening the girls into prostitution; 'care', though nominal, may turn out to have been better than none at all; the 'freedom' of the streets is often the freedom to live or die.

Charities, soup kitchens and hostels may pick up some hapless youngsters and try to filter them through a haphazard rehabilitation system, or 'dry them out' from alcohol or drugs. Older people may get help through organisations like Crisis or the Cyrenians, but evidence suggests that a 'hard-core' of those previously called 'beggars', 'vagrants', or 'of no fixed address' prefer life on the streets to any alternative. Physical and mental health problems are an inevitable long-term result.

Sometimes – just occasionally – there is a relatively 'happy' ending; a young person may see sense, or swallow their pride, or give in to persuasion and return 'home'. The problems which drove them 'away' may not be instantly or permanently solved, but there is at least hope . . .

Travel Now and in the Future

The two following magazine articles, here and on page 185, describe different vehicles either used now or that will be used in the future.

Hey, good-looking

MG's TF will have you wolf-whistling from the rooftops, says **Emma Parker Bowles**

DRIVING A NEW car is like going on a first date. You hope that it's going to be good-looking enough to impress your friends and noisy enough to annoy the neighbours, that it's going to be fun and exciting and that it will leave you wanting more.

Sometimes, it has to be said, a new car is even better than a first date. New cars don't have previous owners to worry about, they don't lie about their mileage, you can leave them outside if you get bored and they don't tell the other cars about your performance.

First impressions are crucial but, of course, it's all a matter of taste. What might make one person's heart beat a little faster might make another reach for the sickbag. My first impressions of the MG TF were good. It wasn't love at first sight but it was handsome enough to be intriguing, sexy enough to put a spring in my step and cute enough to make me want to stroke its bodywork. It is well built and well thought out, managing to look sleek and muscular. My local troupe of all-singing, all-dancing builders was certainly impressed and tore themselves away from their tea break long enough to proclaim it a 'nice snappy little

motor'. This is high praise indeed, as they are notoriously difficult to please. The only other thing that has made them smile recently was watching me, dressed in my pyjamas, chasing my car down the road as it was taken away for its monthly visit to the Chelsea pound.

Rover's MG TF has a reputation to live up to, or even improve upon, as its predecessor, the MGF, has been Britain's bestselling roadster for the past six years. At first glance, MG Rover doesn't seem to have done much more than shove an extra letter in its name, but look closely and the differences become apparent. Its shape is more aerodynamic and less bubble-like than the MGF. More tinker than tailor, more soldier than sailor, it looks a touch tougher and a soupçon more *sportif*.

But looks aren't everything – what of its performance? I can't offer any comparison with the MGF as I have never driven one, but what I can tell you is that it's got plenty of poke and clings to the road as tightly as a supermodel grips her glass of champagne.

Unfortunately, the gearbox is that same supermodel, having guzzled two bottles too many. It can be wantonly disobedient, refusing to do what you want it to.

This minor naughtiness aside, the MG TF is well mannered and easy to get along with. It's as happy nipping about town as it is cruising about the countryside or whipping up the motorway. And there are no nasty surprises, unlike some dates I have been on, which have been truly shocking.

So the TF is good-looking, frisky and fruity. But, just as with people, it's what's on the inside that counts (yeah, right).

For me, the interior of the MG TF was a real let-down, a little like taking off a handsome hunk's clothes to find a nasty pair of Y-fronts. For the price, you ain't never going to get the plushness of a private jet, but you don't want easyJet either. The seats are nice little suede-effect affairs, but I found the dashboard and centre console a bit dull and unimaginative. The cabin's only original, funky element is the gear-stick, although that looks out of place set against the boring buttons and nasty knobs.

Maybe this is nit-picking. It's easy to forgive all these details when, from the outside, it looks so fine and is such fun to drive. A date with an MG TF is one to savour, a nice ride that you won't be embarrassed to tell the girls about. ■

MG TF	
Price £15,750	
Engine 1.8 litre	
Peformance 127mph, 0–60mph in 8.2 seconds	
Colours Pretty much any	
Contact 0845 925 1251	
Bottom line Nicely satisfying	

WRITING ACTIVITY

In groups of two or three, discuss and make notes on the following questions:

The MG TF

1 In what ways does the writer find a new car better than a 'first date'?

2 How are the facts about the MG TF presented?

3 What is the tone of the language used in the article? How does it differ from that of the SoloTrek Flying Vehicle article?

4 Would this article be effective enough to persuade you to purchase an MG TF if you had £16,000 to spend on a car?

SoloTrek Flying Vehicle

1 How does the writer convey the comical aspect of the SoloTrek Flying Vehicle?

2 Which facts show that NASA and the US Department of Defense take it seriously?

3 What information is conveyed about the SoloTrek? What does it consist of and what can it be used for?

4 What in the writer's opinion is the main problem that might be found when using SoloTrek – and how does he suggest that this be solved?

5 What is the style of the language used in the article? Do you think it is appropriate and effective?

6 What extra information or effect does the photograph add?

Need a lift?

The future of commuting starts to take off

The SoloTrek aircraft under test in Sunnydale, California

THERE ARE SEVERAL REASONS why the SoloTrek XFV Exo-Skeletor Flying Vehicle might appear to be no more than a joke. There is its sci-fi name for a start, and the fact that its manufacturer, Millennium Jet of Sunnyvale, California, insists on referring to the device as a 'strap-on'. Its performance in testing seems comical, too: on 18 December last year, it reached a maximum altitude of 24 inches on its maiden, manned flight, which lasted for 19 seconds. It couldn't fly higher because it was tethered to the ground, for safety reasons.

But both NASA and the US Department of Defense take the SoloTrek seriously. The former has so far provided an estimated $6 million of support for its development; and the latter's Defense Advanced Research Projects Agency is currently giving $5 million to fund a three-year testing programme. The US Special Operations Command has even ordered (and paid for) a prototype, which is expected to be delivered next year.

Millennium Jet describes the SoloTrek as a new type of aircraft which will 'take off and land vertically like a helicopter' and 'will transport one individual in an upright and standing position, efficiently, safely and cost-effectively'. Powered by a paraffin-fuelled piston engine, it is expected to have a top speed of 80mph and a range of 130 miles.

The SoloTrek is primarily designed for military applications. But once mass production has been achieved, say its manufacturers, it could be sold at a price 'similar to that of a very high-end sports car'. Clearly some commuters are already thinking of replacing their Ferraris with a faster means of transportation, in fair weather or foul: on of the most frequently asked questions on the SoloTrek website is 'How does the pilot deal with cold weather and rain?'. The answer is with motorcycle clothing.

For more information, go to www.solotrek.com

EXAM PRACTICE ESSAY

After reading the articles on pages 184 and 185, compare their presentation, language and tone. Which do you think is the most effective, and why?

You should include the following in your answer?
- ▶ the detail in the photograph
- ▶ the types of information used
- ▶ facts and opinions
- ▶ the appropriateness of the language to the subject
- ▶ your own response and opinions.

Refer closely to the texts to support your answer.

Coursework

Comparison of a Broadsheet and a Tabloid

Newspaper Article

Newspapers frequently run the same stories, but their presentation, content and the language used often differ considerably. The main story/stories appear on the front page and continue on a later page. The extracts that follow are the first six paragraphs from front page stories and are numbered for use in the activities that follow.

Front page of **Daily Express,** *Friday, April 19 2002*

Hundreds flee horror as plane crashes into packed skyscraper

April 18 2002 Milan

September 11 2001 New York

OH MY GOD NOT AGAIN

FULL STORY & PICTURES PAGES 2&3

OPINION **12** LETTERS **31** DIARY **38** EXPRESS WOMAN **39** TV **49-52** CROSSWORD **53** STARS **54** OBITS **56** CITY **63-67** SPORT **69-80**

Inside page of **Daily Express,** *Friday, April 19 2002*

Five killed as plane flies into packed skyscraper

DEVASTATION: Firefighters and plain clothes police officers race to the area after impact yesterday

i A plane smashed into a Milan sky-scraper yesterday, killing at least five people and injuring scores in a tragedy which revived chilling memories of September 11.

ii One woman leapt to her death as black smoke billowed from the 32-storey building after the propeller-driven light aircraft ploughed into the 25th floor of Italy's landmark Pirelli Tower.

iii Two women passers-by were believed to have been killed by falling debris. Terrified eyewitness Persivale Matteo said last night: 'Everybody feared it was another terrorist attack.'

iv Civil servant Maurizio Sala was on the 20th floor when two explosions shook the building. 'We all rushed to the window and we suddenly realised that it was something similar to the World Trade towers because thousands of pieces of paper were flying through the air. It was the same image,' he said. Military helicopters and jets were scrambled and security forces across the world put on alert.

v But it later emerged that 67-year-old pilot Luigi Fasulo, ... had put out a distress call saying his plane's electrical system had failed.

vi Interior Minister Claudio Scajola confirmed: 'From the information in our possession, we believe it to have been an accident.'

Front page of **The Times**, *Friday, April 19 2002*

'My God, it's like New York all over again'

The gaping hole left in Milan's Pirelli Tower after a single-engined plane crashed into it

From **Richard Owen** in Rome

i STOCK MARKETS and politicians around the world missed a beat last night when a light aircraft crashed into Milan's tallest building.

ii Silvio Berlusconi, the Italian Prime Minister, convened an emergency defence and security meeting after the crash aroused fears of a suicide attack similar to the September 11 attacks in the US. President Bush was informed immediately and stock markets in New York and Frankfurt dropped sharply. But the authorities said they believed the crash was an accident after the pilot had difficulty lowering his undercarriage to land.

iii Reports said that five people had died including the pilot, a 68-year-old Italian named as Luigi Fasulo, who was alone in the aircraft. Police said one woman leapt to her death from the building. 'My God, it's New York all over again,' one bystander said as passers-by covered in blood after being hit by the falling debris were taken to ambulances. Police said there were 'at least 60' people injured.

iv Dozens were injured when fire broke out on two floors of the 417ft Pirelli Tower, which is five miles from the airport where the pilot had been heading. Hours after the crash smoke was rising from the building and liquid was pouring out of a gash in its side.

v The pilot of the Rockwell Commander single-engined plane flying to Milan from Locarno in Switzerland had send a last-minute SOS message reporting problems with the plane's undercarriage before ploughing into the 30-storey tower, which symbolises the city in the heart of the financial and administrative district. It was believed that the pilot, distracted by problems trying to lower the under-carriage, had failed to notice how close he was to the building.

vi Police Officer Celerissimo De Simone said that the pilot of the Rockwell had sent out a distress call at 17.50, just before the crash near the city's main railway station.

Panic after crash, page 5

WRITING ACTIVITY

Looking at the two front pages, and the inside page, copy out and complete the following chart.

FRONT PAGE	THE TIMES	DAILY EXPRESS
size of photographs	third of page	two-thirds of page
size of headlines		
text of headlines		
amount of text in story		
summary of story		
words and phrases used to describe accident		
number of people giving first-person accounts		
facts		
opinions		

Coursework Assignment

Write a comparison of the two articles on the inside page of the *Daily Express* and the front page of the *The Times*, explaining how the two pieces are appropriate for the newspaper for which they are written. The analysis should include:

▶ the use of banner, headlines and captions
▶ the use of photographs
▶ the content
▶ the language used
▶ first-person accounts
▶ fact and opinion.

Before you start writing, you should go back to the beginning of the Media unit on page 154 to remind yourself of the key differences between tabloid and broadsheet newspapers.

SECTION B: WRITING

6 Writing to Argue, Persuade, Advise

Your writing is assessed in the examination and coursework. For one part of your coursework (worth 10%) you will be asked to produce a piece of personal and imaginative writing. All the creative writing activities at the end of the discussion of each poem in Section A, Unit 1 provide suitable assignments.

Here are the other forms of writing that are tested in the examination:

* Writing to Inform, Explain, Describe.
* Writing to Argue, Persuade, Advise.
* Writing to Analyse, Review, Comment.

In all cases you will be set a choice of two questions from which you select **one**. The following three units of the book deal with each of these writing 'triplets' in turn, explaining their key conventions, giving you advice and offering you opportunities for exam practice.

The Specifications

The requirements are the same for both English specifications.

'Writing to Inform, Explain, Describe' is examined in Papers 2F/4H.

'Writing to Argue, Persuade, Advise' and 'Writing to Analyse, Review, Comment, are examined in Papers 3F/5H.

The forms in which your answers are to be written could be any of these: an article, a speech, letter, leaflet or report.

Assessment Objectives

The examiners will be expecting you to communicate clearly and imaginatively, using and adapting forms for different readers and purposes. You will be required to organise your ideas into sentences, paragraphs and whole texts using a variety of linguistic and structural features. You will be further required to use a range of sentence structures effectively with accurate punctuation and spelling.

Part A: Writing to Argue

The word *argue* normally suggests a row or disagreement, where people may shout or lose their tempers. But to *argue a case* for or against something, e.g. banning cigarette advertising, or raising the school leaving age to eighteen, is quite a different process.

1 Firstly, there are always at least *two* sides or viewpoints.

2 Secondly, to argue well, you need to use *evidence* to support your points.

3 Thirdly, your argument needs to be *clear* and *logical*, so that all your points make sense.

ROLE-PLAY

In pairs, choose one of these situations and develop it in a role-play exercise. Use *reasons* to try to win the argument.

1 A teenager wants to go to an all-night party but his or her parents say he or she is too young. They are also worried about the availability of drink and drugs.

2 A customer wants to exchange a sale item that is faulty. The shop assistant says sale items cannot be returned.

3 Two motorists reach the same parking spot at the same time. Each needs to get into town quickly and there is nowhere else to park.

Who *did* win, and *why*?

Write down the *main points* which helped the winner to win.

SPEAKING & LISTENING

In groups of four to six pupils (with both sexes, if you are a coeducational school) discuss which *two* of the following out-of-school activities are most beneficial to teenagers, and why:
  ▶ work in the community, e.g. visiting the elderly or housebound
  ▶ babysitting

> ▷ the Duke of Edinburgh Award Scheme
> ▷ playing a sport
> ▷ dancing.

Elect a group spokesperson and report your group's findings back to the whole class.

Capital Punishment

This is an issue that tends to provoke strong feelings in people. There are a number of countries which still punish some crimes with death (most notably the USA).

So what are the arguments for and against capital punishment? It's best to start with facts about capital punishment as it applies to Great Britain:

Facts

✱ Manslaughter (killing which happened accidentally or in self-defence) resulted in a prison sentence rather than execution.

✱ Anyone convicted of murder but found to be insane would be sent to a top security mental hospital.

✱ Great Britain abolished the death penalty for murder in 1965.

Now let's look at the opinions:

Opinions

✱ Many people think that capital punishment is barbaric and should not be re-introduced.

✱ Others fear that the innocent could be wrongly convicted and executed.

✱ Some people think that, because of increasing violent crime, capital punishment should be re-introduced for murder or terrorism.

For Capital Punishment

Should the Death Penalty be Restored?

Police Federation View*

We have always maintained that capital punishment should be available for the crime of murder. Last year more than 250,000 ordinary members of the public took the trouble to write to us to express their support for the restoration of capital punishment, and we know that many citizens have written to their Members of Parliament asking them to support the restoration of the death penalty.

In the 20 years since abolition, 36 police officers have been killed by criminals in England, Scotland and Wales compared with 12 such deaths in the 20 years before abolition. Each year about 15,000 police officers are assaulted on duty, and about 4,000 sustain injuries which warrant compensation from the Criminal Injuries Compensation Board. In his Annual Report for 1981, the Chief Constable of Strathclyde said that there were 21 attempts to murder police officers in his force. Whilst we recognise that police officers are more likely to find themselves in conflict with criminals, if this is happening to a group which represents no more than one in five hundred of the population, what is happening to the rest? We are particularly concerned about attacks on elderly citizens and lone women.

Terrorism has added an awesome dimension to the question of capital punishment. When the House of Commons voted to abolish capital punishment for a 5-year period in 1965, acts of terrorism in Britain were virtually unknown. The vote to make abolition permanent took place in 1969, just before the present troubles in Northern Ireland degenerated into terrorism. Over the past ten years, the United Kingdom has witnessed terrorism on a scale without precedent in our history. Well over 2,000 people have been killed in Northern Ireland alone, including more than 150 officers serving in the Royal Ulster Constabulary, and more than 400 members of the security forces. Attempts to spread the campaign of bombing and murder to the rest of the United Kingdom have seen the outrages of the Hyde Park and the Regents Park bomb explosions last year, and the Guildford and Birmingham bomb explosions and the attacks on the Tower of London and elsewhere. There have also been deliberate attempts, in some cases successful, to murder prominent persons who were outspoken in their condemnation of terrorism. Members of Parliament will not need to be reminded that two of their colleagues have been assassinated in recent years ...

The overwhelming view of the police service is that capital punishment should be restored for the crime of murder. We accept, of course, that there are degrees of murder and we are not saying that all persons who are convicted of homicide should suffer the death penalty.

Source: The Police Federation, 1986

* N.B. The Police Federation recognises that the restoration of capital punishment is unachievable because, even though the majority of the public are in favour of it, if Parliament tried to re-introduce it, the European Convention on Human Rights would make it unlawful.

Against Capital Punishment

Capital Punishment for Terrorists?

The National Campaign for the Abolition of Capital Punishment sees the problem in the following terms.

- Great Britain has decided, like most countries, that judicial killing has no place in a civilised state, and that this applies to the execution of terrorists as much as to that of any murderer.

- In any case, the practical arguments against executing terrorists are peculiarly strong. Judicial killing is unavoidably slow. There is a preliminary hearing, a trial, usually one or more appeals against conviction; and it can all take many months – in some countries, years. During that time other coercive crimes are likely to happen, including the taking of hostages whose lives will depend on the fate of the prisoner.

- 'Terrorism' today is often the work of minors, female as well as male, whom it would be virtually unthinkable to execute. And the death penalty for terrorists of 'executionable age' might have the ghastly effect of increasing the use of minors for the purpose of homicide.

- Moreover, it makes no sense to kill terrorists whose aims, whatever we think of them, may to them be idealistic, and not to kill those who murder for personal gain.

- Recent years have seen a tragic sequence of convictions against innocent people. With terrorism as with other forms of homicide, there is a constant risk of convictions against innocent people.

- The death penalty, like any other penalty, will deter some killers, but there is no evidence that it does so more than any other. It is in the nature of political 'terrorism' that it is the work of fanatics who accept (indeed sometimes relish) the risk of death 'for the cause'. The judicial killing of terrorists, more often than not, has the opposite effect to that which is intended.

- Reprisals will often follow executions, leading to the loss of still more innocent lives.

Source: NACRO

WRITING ACTIVITY

In pairs, read carefully the two opposing views on capital punishment. Now write two lists, using ideas from the two extracts *and* your own ideas, *for* and *against* capital punishment. Set it out like this:

FOR	AGAINST
1 Killers would hesitate before killing if their own lives were at risk.	1 Executing a killer doesn't bring the dead person back.

Try to get 10 points for each side of the argument. If you have a strong view yourself, try especially hard to see the *other* side and what could be argued in its favour.

Compare your lists with your partner's:
▶ Discuss the differences.
▶ Add to and change your list until you have 10 good points.

Using your final lists, decide on *one* view and write the first draft of a short speech to the class in support of your chosen view.

REMEMBER

✱ Plan your first draft carefully.

✱ Make your points clearly.

✱ Write them in a logical order.

✱ Use both facts and opinions.

✱ Check your work over when you have finished.

You now have your first draft. Look at it again. How can you improve it?

1 Read it to a friend. How did it sound?

2 Listen to his or her comments.

3 Check over your For and Against lists. Are there still some points you didn't use?

4 If so, see if you can fit them in.

Write your second draft and make it longer and stronger! As well as being excellent exam practice, your teacher may decide to hold a class debate on the topic, so your speech could be one of those chosen. If it is, you could also have an oral assessment on it for coursework.

WRITING ACTIVITY

Teenagers are often criticised by adults for things like their:

music (especially its volume!)
hair styles
clothes
friends
habits
untidy rooms
and so on.

Sometimes the criticisms are more serious and include:

drug-taking

graffiti

football hooliganism

rudeness

drinking

smoking

and so on.

When you feel these charges are unjust, you probably try to explain or *argue* against them.

Write a brief (8–10 lines) account of any recent adult criticism and how you dealt with it. Then compare your account with a friend.

EXAM PRACTICE QUESTION

Imagine you read this in the 'Letters to the Editor' page in your local newspaper:

Sir,

I am horrified at the amount of graffiti and vandalism in our town centre. Even the bus shelters are bashed in. None of the public telephones work. Teenagers push and shove their way around, swear loudly and smoke and drink underage. They drop litter and coke cans everywhere and terrify the elderly. Some people I know are afraid to go out at night because of roving teenage gangs. Bring back the birch, the stocks or National Service or lock them up – but do *something* about this badly behaved generation!

Name and address withheld

Write a careful reply, arguing that:
  ▶ Not all teenagers are bad.
  ▶ Many do voluntary service such as visiting the elderly.
  ▶ Graffiti and vandalism are done by a minority.
  ▶ Blaming all teenagers doesn't help.

Also remember to include any other ideas of your own.

Begin your letter, "Sir," and put your name and address or school at the end, if you wish. Why do you think the original writer withheld his or her name and address?

Part B: Writing to Persuade

How good are your powers of persuasion, when you really *want* something?

ROLE-PLAY

In pairs, choose one of these situations and develop it in a role-play exercise.

1 Try to *persuade* a parent to give you:
  ▶ an increase in pocket money
  ▶ your own television
  ▶ a more stylish, expensive mobile phone
  ▶ or some other object of your choice.

Then change roles with your partner and repeat the exercise. How successful were you?

2 You are on the telephone to one of your close friends. Try to persuade him or her to give up one of his or her favourite activities in order to go with you to one of yours, next Saturday.

Then change roles with your partner and repeat the exercise. Which of you was most successful in your persuasion? Why? Jot down a list of 'handy hints' to help you next time.

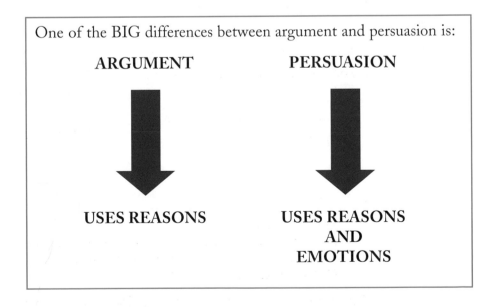

One of the BIG differences between argument and persuasion is:

ARGUMENT   PERSUASION

USES REASONS   USES REASONS
                    AND
                    EMOTIONS

Examples of persuasion (using emotions as well as reasons) are:

- ▶ pleading ('oh, *please*!')
- ▶ threatening ('I'll tell Fred if you don't . . .')
- ▶ blackmail ('But you *promised*!')
- ▶ coercion ('I'd do *anything* for you! You know I would!')
- ▶ fear ('I'd be scared to do it without you!')
- ▶ love ('You're so good to me, I *know* you won't let me down!')

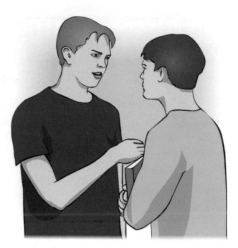

EXAM PRACTICE QUESTION

You see the following advertisement in a newspaper:

Wanted for Americamp 2003: energetic, hardworking, resourceful young people between 15–20 to help run activity holidays for disabled children aged 8–12 years old. This is a wonderful opportunity if you are patient, have a sense of humour and four weeks to spare this summer. Board, lodging and small weekly allowance. Have great fun, help others and make new friends. Write and tell us why this job is for you: Americamp Holidays, 2030 East Twenty-Four Street, New York.

You have nothing arranged for the summer and it will take your mind off waiting for your GCSE results, so you decide to apply. Try to *persuade* them that you are the right kind of person for their camp.

 REMEMBER

- ✱ Plan your letter carefully before beginning.
- ✱ List the things you intend to include such as age, hobbies, and any work experience.
- ✱ Write your letter in paragraphs.
- ✱ Begin with 'Dear Sir or Madam' and end with 'Yours faithfully'.
- ✱ Check your spelling and punctuation.
- ✱ Above all, try to make it a lively, engaging and *persuasive* letter!

Articles

Articles reach a wider audience than you could speak or write to individually, so they can be a useful vehicle of persuasion. But as with any vehicle, some are more powerful than others; due to better design or engineering. As the writer, you are in the 'driving seat' of this 'vehicle', so: 'design' your article well (plan it carefully).

REMEMBER

✴ Check its 'engineering' (shape, form and style).

✴ Have a 'destination' (what you want to achieve) in mind.

✴ 'Drive' there directly and clearly.

Look at this short extract from *The Blue Peter Green Book*.

The Nuclear Debate

Coal, gas and oil will eventually run out and other 'renewable' energy sources have their limitations. So, scientists have looked to nuclear energy which could provide all our needs. To some people, it's the future; to others, it's a world threat. Nuclear energy can be released by a process called nuclear fission which is when unstable atoms that make up things like uranium are split. A chain-reaction occurs which produces enormous amounts of power. In a nuclear reactor, this is controlled to make electricity, but in an atomic bomb it is uncontrolled and causes terrifying destruction. Scientists have also been able to recreate a process called nuclear fusion which is what produces the incredible energy that causes the sun and stars to shine. But so far they've only harnessed it for destruction, the deadly hydrogen bomb. Fusion energy has yet to be tamed to produce electricity.

Campaigners against nuclear weapons are horrified that we have created weapons, capable of destroying the world, in the name of 'peace'. In the 1960s they formed a protest organisation called The Campaign for Nuclear Disarmament (CND) which has been fighting ever since under the banner 'Ban the Bomb'. Campaigners against nuclear-generated electricity are worried about the potentially dangerous radioactive waste produced by nuclear power stations and the risk of accidents. They argue that high-level radioactive waste remains a threat to people for hundreds, possibly thousands, of years so safe storage can't be guaranteed. They also argue that accidents in America and Russia prove that nuclear power isn't as safe as is claimed.

Supporters of nuclear weapons believe that the fear that they could be used has prevented another major world war, like the Second World War. That war ended when two atomic bombs were dropped by America on the Japanese cities of Hiroshima and Nagasaki in 1945, killing more than 200,000 people and causing widespread destruction.

Supporters of nuclear-generated electricity argue that it is a relatively clean, safe, efficient way of making electricity. They say it causes less damage to the environment than burning fossil fuels; that more people die from air pollution caused by coal than from nuclear accidents or the small amounts of potentially dangerous radioactive waste produced by nuclear fission. Nuclear power provides about 20% of Britain's electricity, and about 70% in France.

Now look at it again. You will notice that it has a certain form to it:

Paragraph 1: gives basic facts about energy, especially nuclear power.
Paragraph 2: gives the arguments *against* the use of nuclear power.
Paragraphs 3 and 4: give the arguments *for* both nuclear weapons and using nuclear power.

WRITING ACTIVITY

A nuclear power station with research facilities is to be built near your home. Using the information in the extract, and any other ideas of your own, write an article for a local magazine, either supporting or opposing the project.
▶ Write between 500–700 words.
▶ Make your article as persuasive as possible.

WRITING ACTIVITY

Read the following article about Kelly Smith, an England women's football star.

Using the information and other ideas of your own, write a positive, enthusiastic article for your school magazine to persuade more girls to take up football.

REGIMEN

Kelly Smith, 23, footballer, England's women's team

Weight: 10st
Height: 5ft 6in

As the David Beckham of women's football, what are the demands of your star status?
I don't have it as bad as Beckham, but the media has increased its demands for interviews. After games we have to spend at least half an hour signing autographs.

What sort of training helps you score goals?
Repetition, I do a lot of finishing drills. We train for about two hours a day five times a week, lifting weights twice a week. I practise taking penalties – the key is to choose your spot and not change your mind.

You play your club football in America. Has this been good for your football career?
It's great because it's the only country to have a professional league where I'm playing with international players.

Does your club, Philadelphia Charge, train as hard as a men's team?
Of course we do. The season runs from March to August; for the rest of the year I work out with a fitness coach three times a week.

Are you on a special diet?
No, we are old enough to take care of our bodies and eat properly. If I have a weakness it's Cadbury's Whole Nut.

How important is your weight?
Weight is not an issue with me. I don't count calories and I don't know how it affects my game.

What difference does the playing surface make to your game?
A big difference. Last year our home field was AstroTurf and everyone hated it. This year we have new synthetic grass, which is more like real grass but not as unpredictable.

Do you encounter disdainful comments from men about women's football?
Only in England. That's why I live in the US; I hate those comments. They are nearly all from men who haven't seen a proper professional women's game. I feel sorry for them.

Do you think that the England women's team stand more or less chance of becoming world champs than the men's team?
Less. We are still trying to get recognition in England. But the women's game is improving. ●

Nick Wyke

Part C:) Writing to Advise

How many times have you been given *advice* you didn't want, especially by interfering friends or adults? How often have you been asked to *advise* someone else? Have you given good, clear, fair advice?

ROLE-PLAY

1 Role-play a situation with a friend. One of you has a school-based problem (e.g. about an academic subject or a friendship group) and confides in the other person, who then gives advice.

2 Then reverse the roles, with another school problem.

3 Now discuss the outcomes:
  ▶ How did each of you decide what advice to give?
  ▶ How did you each react to the advice given?

4 Write a brief list of what makes good advice, e.g. should it always be kind, or frank, or definite?

5 Compare lists. How many things did you agree on? Where did you differ?

WRITING ACTIVITY

Now, think of some professional advice-givers and their roles. Try to fill in the empty spaces in the table below.

ADVISER	AREA OF ADVICE	METHODS USED
Agony Aunt or Uncle in a magazine	Personal problems of various kinds.	Answer in letters page; usually sympathetic.
Policeman or Policewoman		
Careers Officer		
Lawyer		
Teacher		
Social Worker		
Civil Servant (e.g. to an MP)		

Question: How many different kinds of advice are there?
Answer: Many!

✱ Some advice is purely practical (e.g. how to protect your house from burglary).

✱ Some is factual (e.g. the qualifications for a particular career or college).

✱ Some is of a more personal nature (e.g. how to stop biting your nails).

WRITING ACTIVITIES

1 Imagine that you have a young cousin called Lucy. She is seven and a half years old and has always looked up to you, almost embarrassingly at times. You are clearly her hero or heroine! Your name is Samuel or Samantha, as the case may be. A few days after Christmas you receive this letter from Lucy:

> Boxin Day
>
> Dear Cosin Sam,
>
> I hope you had a nice chrismas and LOTS of presants. I didn't cos I found out something reeley orfull. My borther tolld me. Theres no Farther Cristmas. I cryed and cryed.
>
> Mummy said it was true. So I cryed some more. It was horrid. My pressents don't seam so nice now I no they didn't come from Farther Cristmas. Can you help? No won ellse understands.
>
> Luv
> Lucy
> (aged 7 and a half)

Write your reply. Remember, however, that:
▶ she is clearly distressed
▶ she is very young (as her spelling shows)
▶ she looks up to you.

Decide how honest you are going to be and how you are going to word your reply. Try to use:
▶ a fairly simple vocabulary
▶ short rather than long sentences.

Above all, try to make her feel *better* not worse, even if you do confirm her worst fears!

2 A friend of your own age, who has since gone to another school outside your area, writes and tells you about several problems at home. She is unhappy enough to seriously think of running away. Write a reply advising her not to do anything that she might later regret.

Before you begin, decide:

▷ what her problems are
▷ why it might not be a good idea for her to run away
▷ what else she could do
▷ what you would do in that situation.

FURTHER ACTIVITIES

1 Think of a typical teenage problem (e.g. about relationships of one sort or another, appearance, self-confidence, etc.). Try to think yourself into the mind of a person who has this problem. Write 'their' letter to a popular problem page in a magazine for 14–18 year olds.

Change letters with a partner. Each of you write a 'reply' to the other's letters.

2 Now, examine the reply you received.

Was it:
✳ What you might have expected?
✳ Kind and helpful?
✳ Or unkind and unhelpful?

Did it:
✳ Make good suggestions you hadn't thought of?
✳ Seem a realistic response to the problem?
✳ Show understanding?

Discuss your answers with your partner, and see what you have both learnt from the experience.

3 The Head Teacher has asked Year 11 students to prepare an Advice Sheet for next year's incoming Year 7, on all aspects of school life. The intention is to help them to fit in and find their way round the school routines as quickly as possible. The Head suggested:

▷ Putting the advice under different sub-headings, such as: Games, Homework, Lunches, Rules, Clubs and Activities, etc.
▷ Keeping it easy to understand.
▷ Making helpful suggestions of things you have found useful yourself.
▷ Answering questions that Year 7 students might ask.
▷ Putting in any visual material, e.g. maps, you think necessary.

Bearing this advice in mind and thinking back to your own experiences in Year 7:

▷ Make a plan of what you are going to include.
▷ How you are going to organise it.
▷ Any visual material to be used.

Compare your plan with a friend's to see if you have left out anything vital. Then you can begin writing!

4 It is spring again and people are thinking about their summer holidays. The police are thinking too – about the number of avoidable burglaries when families leave their homes unattended for a fortnight. They decide to issue an advice leaflet to householders explaining what precautions they should take before leaving.

The Chief Constable wants to raise crime awareness in the area, so he organises a competition for the best leaflet in local secondary schools. You and your friends decide to enter.

Begin by making a list of points to include, and ways of illustrating them such as:

Cancel all milk and papers.

When you have finished your list, think of a good title for the leaflet, such as:

Watch out, there's a thief about!

or

Beat the Burglars this Summer!

Then, decide on your layout, and write your leaflet.

Consider the following police guidelines when you are writing your leaflet.

* Write simply and clearly.

* Use pictograms as well as words.

* Remember that some people can't read small print.

* Not everyone has English as their first language.

* Make them eye-catching.

* Use bullet points or short paragraphs.

7 Writing to Inform, Explain, Describe

Writing to Inform

How often have you been asked to give information, explain a point or a process or describe a place, person or an event?

The answer is probably, more times than you can remember! We are *always* doing these things voluntarily, as well as being *asked* to do them by friends, family and teachers.

How often have you been stopped in the street and asked for directions? Have you ever realised afterwards that you gave the wrong information?

ROLE-PLAY

In pairs, practise giving information by doing the following activities.

1 *Tell* a friend how to get to your home from school; then reverse roles. If you already know your friend's route, comment on the accuracy of the information he or she gave and suggest any ways in which it could have been improved or made easier to follow.

2 *Inform* your friend how you spent last weekend. Try to make your account clear, vivid and lively. Then reverse roles and listen to his or her account. Ask for any further information (within reason!) which will help to make events clearer, e.g. 'What kind of music did they play?', 'How many people were there?', 'What time did you go home?', and so on.

WRITING ACTIVITIES

1 In your role-play you will have discovered that providing information effectively involves:
  ▶ being concise
  ▶ including only relevant information
  ▶ ensuring that your information is clear and unambiguous
  ▶ predicting likely questions or difficulties and dealing with them
  ▶ using language that your audience understands.

All these are also features of good *writing* to inform. However, writing involves a number of additional features that you will need to bear in mind.

Read the example below which is taken from the introduction of a sports and social club website.

The desire to do something a little out of the ordinary, is in all of us don't you think? But it is very seldom achieved – how many times have you said 'I would love to have a go at that BUT . . .'? Now there is an organisation that can help you Live Your Dream . . .

SPICE was set up over fourteen years ago in Manchester, to cater for members who are ordinary everyday people . . . but want to do extraordinary things in their spare time. Things like WHITE WATER RAFTING, FIRE EATING, HOT AIR BALLOONING, ABSEILING, TIGHT ROPE WALKING and many many more. In short, people who wanted to add a little SPICE to life, that extra magic ingredient. There are also the more usual activities – each month groups go off to the theatre, cinemas, wine tasting – or a look behind the scenes of a newspaper publishers, down the local sewers, driving buses on skid pans, wing walking, and the list goes on . . .

Source: www.spiceuk.com/intro

How might the website continue to inform readers about the club? With a partner, make a list of the information that people might need to know before they join, for example membership details, opening hours and so on.

When you have completed your list, choose two sections to write in detail.

 REMEMBER

* Keep your information:
  ▷ clear
  ▷ relevant
  ▷ direct

2 Now look at the following extract from a tourist guide to York.

Tourist shopping

Despite York residents' moans about the city centre being turned into a 'visitors museum', there is plenty of shopping activity. Naturally, tourist shops are plentiful, although some of them seem to have a fairly short life. Good tourist shopping streets are The Shambles (once the haunt of butchers' shops – look out for the broad shop window ledges), High and Low Petergate and Stonegate. And don't forget the ultimate place for morning coffee or afternoon tea: Betty's Tearooms St Helen's Square, York. Tel: 01904 889822.

Source: www.cityofyork.com

a) You will notice that, as well as providing information, the writer has taken care to present the information in a lively style. With a partner, note down examples of humour and figurative language and explain how they improve the effectiveness of the writing.

b) You have been doing a combined History and Geography project on your local area. Using what you have learnt, write an interesting and *informative* leaflet on the locality for visitors. Include amenities and recreation, sites or museums worth visiting, and any other aspects of the area you think important.

REMEMBER

✱ Select your material carefully.

✱ Use sub-headings (e.g. 'Local Industry', 'Entertainments', and so on).

✱ Write in a lively style.

✱ Use any relevant illustrations, (e.g. maps, photographs and old pictures).

Part B: Writing to Explain

Explaining something should be easy when you really understand it. But is it? If you have a younger brother or sister, try to remember the last time you explained something to them. Were you successful? Did they really understand your explanation?

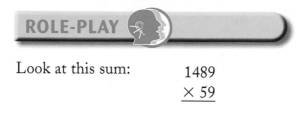

ROLE-PLAY

Look at this sum:

$$1489$$
$$\times\ 59$$
$$\overline{}$$

Your younger brother or sister has been told to do the sum for homework, without using a calculator. Explain to them how to do it. Begin: 'First you . . .', until you arrive at the answer, 87,851. The important thing here is to explain *how* to do it. This is called explaining a process.

WRITING ACTIVITIES

1 Now try a little experiment in groups of four to six:
   ▷ Send one person out of the room for 5 minutes. A second member of the group should *silently* and slowly demonstrate an everyday process, such as tying a shoelace or a tie.
   ▷ The rest of the group should write down each stage of the demonstration process. They may ask for a part to be repeated again, if necessary.
   ▷ When everyone has finished their lists of how to do it, call in the person from outside.
   ▷ Ask him or her to simply follow, using the tie or shoe, a student's explanation of how to tie it. It is important that the explanation as read out is followed strictly.
   ▷ Try out one or two other explanatory lists to see if they are as or more accurate.
   ▷ Then decide, as a group, what you have learnt from this activity.

2 Students are often quite lost when it comes to domestic skills, once they have left home and gone to university or college. Imagine you are a second-year student living in a self-catering hall of residence. The Warden has asked a group of you to help prepare a basic survival sheet, called 'Making the Break: Leaving Home and Becoming a Student', aimed at first-year students.

It needs to include the following sub-headings:

✱ 'How to Live on £50 a Week' (e.g. divided up between food, clothes, books, transport, entertainment).

✱ 'Making Healthy Meals Cheaply'.

✱ 'Simple Snacks' (e.g. how to make an omelette, beans on toast, scrambled eggs, and so on).

✱ 'Getting to Grips with the Work' (e.g. planning, researching, giving it in on time, and so on).

✱ 'Joining Clubs, Interest Groups and College Teams'.

✱ 'Using the Student Bar Sensibly'.

Choose any two topics from the list and explain what you think new students need to know about them.

! REMEMBER

✱ Include as much detail as necessary.

✱ Try to write in a lively, interesting style.

✱ Make it clear that, although being a student is a serious business, it is also fun.

3 Each member of your class has been asked to give a 3 to 5 minute talk on a hobby or sport they enjoy.
▶ First, choose your topic.
▶ Then write your talk, explaining its main attractions, and why you like it.
▶ Now time yourself reading your talk aloud to a small group.

If it is only between 1½ to 2 minutes long when reading at your normal speaking pace, see if you can:
▶ Add more to your existing material.
▶ Or add *new* material (e.g. equipment needed, or rules of the game).

When you have extended its length to 3 minutes or more, try and *reduce* it to a series of headings and sub-headings on a postcard, as below:

Why I Love Cricket

DAD: Played; taught me; first bat for my fourth birthday; the GOOGLY!; broken windows . . .

SCHOOL: Teams; matches; First Eleven; County under-13s.

COUNTY/TEST CRICKET: "Boring game"? No! *Very* exciting! Lords; Old Trafford visits . . .

MY FAVOURITE CRICKETERS: My Dad! Shane Warne; Imran Khan; Viv Richards; WG Grace.

MY AMBITION: To play for England!

4 You have been asked to be part of a survey on young people's attitudes to various things. Each week you are sent two topics or statements and asked to give your views on them. This week you are being asked to:

▶ Explain, as fully as possible, your views on marriage and family life, including how you see your own future.

▶ Respond to this statement: 'Young people are not as concerned about the effects of drugs, drink and Aids as they should be.' (You may agree or disagree, or a bit of both, but are asked to explain your reasons for your views).

Prepare your answers carefully, as you think you would send them in to the survey. You may wish to discuss the issues briefly in groups of three before beginning, to help you sort out your own views.

Part C: Writing to Describe

Everyone can describe things, but how well can you do it? Can you really bring things to life for other people? Can you help them to see through your eyes, people they've never met, or places they've never been? Let's see.

Describing People

WRITING ACTIVITIES

1 Describe yourself, as you might to a new pen friend when no up-to-date photograph is available. As well as your appearance, try to include your personality. Write six to eight lines, choosing your adjectives carefully.

Now show your self-description to a friend and ask them how accurate they think it is. Would they know it was you, if you hadn't said? Did you give enough precise details?

Read the following description of Niang from *Chinese Cinderella* then think of a person you know well, but preferably not someone in the classroom.

'Our step-mother, whom we called Niang, was a seventeen-year-old Eurasian beauty fourteen years his junior. Father always introduced her to his friends as his French wife though she was actually half French and half Chinese. . . . She was almost as tall as Father, stood very straight and dressed only in French clothes – many of which came from Paris. Her thick, wavy, black hair never had a curl out of place. Her dark-brown eyes were fringed with long, thick lashes. She wore heavy make-up, expensive French perfume and many diamonds and pearls.'

Source: Chinese Cinderella by Adeliune Yen Mah

If they went missing and the police asked you for a description, what would you say?

▶ Start off by establishing some basic facts in the table below:

hair colour	
hair style	
height	
build	
eye colour	
complexion	
freckles, glasses, dimples, beards, etc.	
usual clothes	

▶ Now, try to put these facts together into two or three sentences.

▶ How carefully did you choose your adjectives? As an exercise, list 25 different words which could describe hair (include colours, styles, types).
Here are three to start you off: ginger, short, curly.

▶ When you have written as many as you can, compare your list with a friend's.

▶ What did you leave out?

▶ Did you include, for example, receding, bald, fly-away or plaited? If not, add them in your list.

▶ Then consider the person's personality (e.g. are they kind, humorous, sulky, quiet, chatty, and so on).

▶ Add a further two or three sentences covering personality, then look at your whole description.

▶ Does it seem fairly accurate? Is there anything vital you have left out? If so, add it in your description.

4 Imagine you have been selected to be a contestant on the television show, *Blind Date*. You have been asked to give a brief description (about six to eight lines) of your ideal boyfriend/husband or girlfriend/wife. Think carefully about their physical and mental characteristics, abilities and interests, and choose your adjectives as accurately as you can.

5 Study these two paintings:

a) 'The Girl with the Pearl Earring' by Vermeer, dated 1665
b) 'A Bar at the Folies-Bergère' by Manet, dated 1881–1882.

Both are of young women, one Dutch, one French, and have been painted two hundred years apart. The painting by Vermeer includes the girl's head and shoulders only, on a dark background, so all the emphasis is on her expression. Whereas Manet's painting focuses on the barmaid but includes her back view in the mirror, the details of the bar and the reflection of the customers at the 'Folies-Bergère' (a kind of night-club with a floor-show in Paris).

Look again at the girl in Vermeer's painting. Describe, as fully as possible:
▶ her appearance, clothes and jewellery
▶ the colour scheme
▶ her facial expression (What are her eyes and mouth saying? What might she be feeling or thinking?).

Try out various adjectives to capture her expression. Is she shy, innocent, amused or something else entirely?

When you have finished, compare notes with a partner. Have you said the same or quite different things? There is no 'right' or 'wrong' description, it is what *you* think, and what matters is that it is as well-expressed as you can make it.

Now look again at Manet's painting. It is much fuller and more detailed, so your description will have to be, too. Use the three points mentioned previously but add a fourth:
▶ Describe her surroundings and the use of perspective (what is near and what is in the distance).

Again, try out various adjectives to capture the young woman's facial expression (Is she sad, upset, puzzled or something else entirely?).

When you have finished your second description, compare the two:
▶ Which was easiest?
▶ Which do you think you did best?
▶ Do you feel that you said all you could?
▶ Are you beginning to choose your words more carefully?
▶ How many drafts did you do?

WRITING BASED ON THE PICTURE

Use the picture you prefer as the basis for a piece of writing, telling the 'story' behind the picture and the girl's expression.

Describing Places

Places are almost as important in our lives as people. They take on special meanings for us; in some we feel instantly 'at home', in others we are never relaxed and comfortable. We are territorial like animals and need our own space where we feel able to be 'ourselves'.

WRITING ACTIVITIES

1 Look at the following example of a personified description:

'I came upon a boiler wallowing in the grass, then found a path leading up the hill. It turned aside for the boulders, and also for an undersized railway-truck lying there on its back with its wheels in the air. One was off. The thing looked as dead as the carcass of some animal. I came upon more pieces of decaying machinery, a stack of rusty nails.'

Conrad, *Heart of Darkness*

Pick out the words which show that the boiler and the railway truck are being described as though they are people or animals. This is not how we expect things to be described, so it surprises us and makes ordinary things seem strange.

2 The following description is of an aerial view of a landscape with houses, a railway line, boats on the water and a road with cars:

'Bond had a moment of exhilaration as the sun came up. Twenty thousand feet below, the houses began to show like grains of sugar spilt across a brown carpet. Nothing moved on the earth's surface except a thin worm of smoke from a train, the straight white feather of a fishing boat's wake across an inlet, and the glint of chromium from a toy motor car caught in the sun.'

Ian Fleming, *Diamonds are Forever*

> Pick out one simile that describes the houses.
> Pick out two metaphors that describe train smoke and a boat's wake.
> Explain why the car is referred to as 'a toy motor.'
> Are these similes and metaphors good descriptions of an aerial view? Do they help you to picture it?

Describing Things

Everyday objects which we take for granted are not as easy to describe as you would think.

WRITING ACTIVITIES

1 As a warm-up exercise try describing one of these following things to an imaginary Martian who has no idea what you're talking about:

a saucepan
a toothbrush
a fried egg
a television
a GameBoy

In each case, describe the shape, size, colour, material, what it does and how you use it.

Not so easy, was it? How many times did you change your description, or start again?

2 Now look at the opening paragraph of *Unicorn Summer*, a historical novel by Rhona Martin:

showing no mercy

blessing

metaphor

soft, rippling sound

suggests exposure and vulnerability

so wet!

All day it had rained. Not the soft benison of summer rain lisping gently from leaf to leaf, but bitter needles of sleet that drove relentlessly down between naked branches to beat on the forest floor, stitching black leaves of winter to the iron ground. The natural sounds of the greenwood were stilled. Fox and badger stayed snug in their earths, deer stood silent and dispirited. Even the birds found little to say, their occasional voices drowned by the incessant drumming of the rain.

links to 'needles'

stresses hardness of winter

unending rhythm of the rain

animals holed-up or miserable

This is a beautifully crafted piece of writing, where everything hangs together to give a vivid picture of winter and the vicious, driving rain. Few of us can write this well, but there's no harm in trying!

▶ Try to write a similar paragraph, using at least one simile or metaphor, about a scorchingly hot summer.
▶ Try to make your descriptions: vivid, colourful, exact, amusing and memorable. Quite a tall order!

REMEMBER:

Similes and metaphors both compare two dissimilar things, but similes use *like* or *as* and metaphors just say one thing *is* another, for example:

* Simile: 'The road was *like* a ribbon of moonlight over the purple moor.'

* Metaphor: 'The road *was* a ribbon of moonlight over the purple moor.'

3 Why do we need similes and metaphors at all? Compare these two sentences:
   a) 'Come down here at once!' my mother shouted.
   b) 'Come down here at once!' my mother squawked like an angry parrot.

   Which one is more lively and colourful? The sentence including the simile! That's why we need them.

4 What makes a good simile or metaphor? Look at these two examples and see how effective you think they are:
   a) 'The keyboard of the old piano looked like a mouthful of rotten teeth.'
   b) 'The keyboard of the piano looked like a mouthful of bad teeth, chipped, yellow, and some missing altogether' (Leslie Thomas, *This Time Next Week*).

   Does the greater detail in example **b)** make it a better simile, or is it too long?

5 Write a short, descriptive paragraph on one of these subjects, using *one* good simile:
   ▶ a derelict (ruined) house
   ▶ a cold night by the river
   ▶ an early morning street market
   ▶ a burst water main in a busy street.

   Were you pleased with your simile? Compare it to a friend's and decide which one you both prefer and why.

6 Now you have had some practice writing short descriptions you will be ready to try one of the following activities that require longer descriptions.
   ▶ Describe one of your favourite places, so that others could picture it easily.
   ▶ Describe your ideal home.
   ▶ Describe a place where you felt distinctly ill-at-ease or uncomfortable.

REMEMBER

* Try not to use similes or metaphors that you've heard before. Try to think up your own, or change an existing one, e.g. 'The road was a green snake twisting over the purple moor', is still better than just saying, 'The road twisted across the purple moor'.

* Avoid over-used, meaningless adjectives, such as: wonderful, marvellous, nice, nasty, pretty, terrible, dreadful, lovely, tremendous, and so on. Also avoid using made-up words, such as 'ginormous' and 'humungous'.

UNIT 8 Writing to Analyse, Review, Comment

Part A: Writing to Analyse

The word *analyse* is often associated with science subjects such as chemistry, but you can also analyse a character's motives, a set of statistics, or the ingredients in a recipe. For the purposes of the exam, it often means investigating opposite viewpoints, such as the advantages and disadvantages of a situation. For example, would it be better to fly–drive to the south of France or go by train and boat? Both would have their pros and cons.

ROLE-PLAY

In pairs, discuss a situation of conflict or disagreement in any book or play you are reading for GCSE (e.g. in *Romeo and Juliet*, Act 3, Scene 5 where Juliet is told by her father that she has to marry Paris against her wishes). Try to *analyse* the motives of each of the characters, (e.g. who do you think has the strongest case in the disagreement) and why the 'winner' wins.

WRITING ACTIVITIES

1 Look at the following advertisement for a Subaru Legacy Estate 2.0 and try to analyse how it is being marketed as a sports car.

You should mention:
▶ the main title
▶ the road angle of the car
▶ the use of rhyme, dashes and double meanings
▶ special features
▶ phrasing (e.g. why 'All-Wheel Drive' instead of '4-Wheel drive'?)
▶ use of lists
▶ layout.

✱ How successful do you think this advert will be?

✱ Would you be tempted to road-test or buy this car if you were older and could afford it? Why, or why not?

2 Monarch or President? Much has been said, argued and written about whether or not Great Britain should still have a Royal Family. The death of the Queen Mother in 2002 aged 101, raised many of those issues again. Read the article, which gives the 'Mirror Mailbox' readers' views. The Letters Editor has clearly tried to give a balance of views between the two sides.

▷ Analyse the 'Yes' and 'No' letters into two lists of main points, in the same way as you would for a debate.

▷ Then use the information to write an article entitled 'Monarch or President?' aimed at the readers of *The Mirror* magazine.

⊘ REMEMBER

✳ Give a balance of views.

✳ Structure your article carefully.

✳ Include an introduction and a conclusion.

✳ Make your article informative and interesting.

THE MIRROR, *Thursday, April 11, 2002*

Mirror M@ilbox

Edited by
**GERRIE
ESAU**

HAVE YOUR SAY: Write to Letters Editor, The Mirror, One Canada Square, London E14 5AP
email: mailbox@mirror.co.uk Fax: 020 8293 3975 *Letters and email must include your full postal address. We reserve the right to edit your letters*

Has your faith in the crown been restored?

THE nation's reaction to the Queen Mother's death has proved that we do hold the royal family in high esteem (The Mirror, April 10).

It has also shown just how important our monarchy actually is.

This bond must not be broken by allowing so many hangers-on to take taxpayers' money and do nothing in return.

The Queen, Princess Anne and Prince Charles work tirelessly but too many members of the family do not – their financial support should be cut off.

Nigel Abbott, Chester

YES

● We have been shown just how important it is to have a monarchy. If we were to dispose of it how would we select the Queen's replacement?

We certainly don't want a retired politician, boring academic, Flash Harry businessman or media star to represent our great country.

Elected presidents are more concerned with their own political futures and powers. We are better off with our royal family – don't give up something that works so well.

**J B Ogilvie
Sherborne, Dorset**

● People worry that joining the euro would mean Britain losing its identity. But Tuesday showed the world what it means to be British and just how great the nation is because of our royals.

**Elaine Cheetham
Cardiff**

● Our monarchy represents more than 1,000 years of history and heritage, and is still envied by much of the world.

If you take it away, Britain will become just another faceless state with no real identity.

J Wilkin, by email

● It would be a very sad day if the monarchy were to be dissolved.

Let's hope the Queen Mother's death does reignite the British people's faith and love for it.

The House of Windsor has experienced many problems – this is family life – but our Queen reigns with dignity and courage.

**M Elliott
Dewsbury, West Yorks**

● Those against the monarchy seem to think its end will usher in a golden age of equality.

In fact, Britain would have a US-style president.

His or her lifestyle would be as costly as a monarch's and every five years we taxpayers will have to fork out for an election.

**Victoria Hastings
Sandwich, Kent**

● Yes, we need our royal family but perhaps in a slightly different form.

I live in Spain now, and its royals – who command great respect from the people – have far fewer hangers-on.

Perhaps ours should thin down a bit, too.

Richard Worden, by email

● If the rest of the family had performed as well as our Queen Mother, there wouldn't be so many anti-monarchists now.

**J H Vincent
Goonhavern, Cornwall**

NO

● The Queen Mother's death is another nail in the coffin lid for the monarchy.

If anything, the pomp and ceremony surrounding her funeral has highlighted the huge gap between the rich and the poor in this country.

Thousands upon thousands of our senior citizens are living in poverty or near the breadline, receiving less than £6,000 a year in state pensions, yet an obscene amount of money was spent on her funeral.

It's time the outdated monarchy called it a day.

Gary Read, Manchester

● The Queen Mother's funeral has been the perfect reminder of the vast inequality in class and distribution of wealth that the lamented Elizabeth sadly represented.

**Joseph Doran
Archway, North London**

● Rather than cementing the monarchy, I feel the Queen Mother's death will be the end as there is nobody to replace her.

The Queen works hard but when she eventually steps down all we are left with is an over-privileged family who have contributed nothing to society.

J Thompson, by email

● The Queen Mother is dead – Long Live the Revolution.

We cannot afford the luxury of a royal family and the obscene amount of money that must have been spent on the Queen Mother's funeral would have been better given to the NHS to help other elderly people.

**Katherine Allatt
Northampton**

● We really don't need this spectacle of pomp and ceremony.

The end to this farce of our royal family is long overdue.

**G Hetherington
Harrington, Cumbria**

● People will say that the spin off from the royals prancing around the country benefits the economy and brings in tourism.

Well it doesn't benefit my economy. As an OAP I see no return at all.

**P W Lyons
Portsmouth, Hampshire**

● The conclusion to your article Voice of The Mirror said that the monarchy was now safe forever (*The Mirror*, April 10). What absolute cobblers.

There may be a lot of emotion at the moment because the Queen Mother has died but you try testing the water in a couple of months when the Wessexes have cancelled a few engagements, and Prince Philip has found someone else to insult and see how popular they are then.

**Ian Powell
Whitburn, Tyne and Wear**

Part B: Writing to Review

To review is to consider or reflect on something, such as a play, a situation, an event, or someone's conduct. Professional reviewers are also critics: they attempt to assess the value of a film, or the virtues of a singer, and to pass judgements on how good things are.

'I am reviewing the situation – I think I'd better think it out again!' sang Fagin towards the end of *Oliver*.

ROLE-PLAY

In pairs, practise your reviewing skills by choosing one of these situations and developing it into a role-play exercise.

1 Think of a time in your own life when you have *reviewed* a situation, then re-thought things. Outline the example, then tell your partner what you feel you learned from it.

2 Try to remember an incident which was awkward or embarrassing at the time, but which you later realised had a funny side. Tell this to your partner, explaining how this realisation changed your view of the incident.

WRITING ACTIVITIES

1 Think about books, plays, films, TV programmes, new CDs or DVDs: why do people review them?
   ▶ Write a list of possible reasons, such as: to give information to the public.
   ▶ Then compare your list with a partner. How many points did you get between you? How many were the same?
   ▶ Who reads reviews, for example, in newspapers or magazines like *The New Musical Express*? Have you ever read one yourself? If so, did it influence you?
   ▶ Have you ever been asked to write a review, for example, for a school newsletter?

2 Try to remember your school's last production of a play, musical, fashion show or festival. Imagine you have been asked to review the event in the school newsletter.

You should mention:
   ▶ when and what it was
   ▶ who was in it and how they performed
   ▶ the stage sets, costumes, music and lighting
   ▶ any particularly memorable moments
   ▶ the production team
   ▶ special effects (if any)
   ▶ anything else which adds interest.

3 Professional reviewers can be:
▶ neutral (or non-critical)
▶ biased in favour
▶ biased against.

Often they mix their comments, so that readers can see both sides and then make up their own minds. Some of the best reviews have a gently amused tone. Read the review below of the school-based play, *Daisy Pulls It Off*, set in 1927, but first performed in 1983, then revived in 2002. Then answer the questions on page 226.

THE TIMES WEDNESDAY MAY 1 2002

Jolly good return to an age that never was

Theatre

Daisy Pulls It Off

Lyric, Shaftesbury Avenue

★★★★☆

Benedict Nightingale

WE LIVE in sad, cynical times. If someone asked you to see a play called *Daisy Pulls It Off* at the south end of Soho today, you might conclude that the correct dress for the occasion would be a dirty mac. But tweeds, brogues and an old school tie are the most suitable wear for audiences of either gender. Denise Deegan's delightful comedy pulls us back into an era when girls – sorry, gels – were learning the meaning of patriotism and empire on the playing fields of Roedean.

OK, the public school where the play is set is called Grangewood but, since the heroine pluckily rescues a couple of fellow pupils from a collapsing cliff, it clearly has a coastal site in common with that great academy. Deegan also helps to explain why Katherine Whitehorn, a Roedean alumna, once responded to a request for money by saying that she hoped the dear old place would fall into the sea. She was no good at games and so fulfilled Daisy Meredith's best friend's definition of a 'rotter'.

Still, that was long ago, and the year when Hannah Yelland's bright, eager Daisy comes to Grangewood is even longer ago: 1927. That's not so good for her, since she's a scholarship girl from

an elementary school and, therefore, innately offensive to the likes of Jane Mark's Sybil and her toadying sidekick, Anna Francolini's Monica. It doesn't help that Daisy is brilliant at work, stunning at games, plucky, modest, and as good an egg as any since Humpty Dumpty.

This snobbish, hockey-hating duo frame her as a cheat, thief and sneak. And do they get her expelled? That's a pretty silly question when the head of the school is Katherine Igoe's ripping Clare Beaumont, on whom everyone has a pash, and Clare's No 2 is Emma Stanfield's genially butch hockey captain, who says things like 'nil desperandum, me darling'. Angela Brazil's novels, which Deegan is parodying yet celebrating, tend not to end with nice, sporty gels forced to do awful things, like become prostitutes or governesses, to survive.

I was a games-shunning rotter at

my alma mater, and, when enjoined to have more 'school spirit', I tended to replenish my hidden cache of gin; yet I found myself drawn into a tale whose glorious implausibilities include hidden treasure and a 'dead' father stricken with amnesia. I was fascinated by the tension between group loyalty, which means that grassing is the crime of crimes, and the need to expose serious wrongdoing. I was entranced by the slang: 'brekkers', 'new bug', etc. I was filled with nostalgia for an England that has never existed: jolly decent, jolly confident, jolly innocent and crammed with young ladies in gymslips.

As staged by David Gilmore, who directed the play's original production 19 years ago, it makes a topping holiday from twenty-first century reality. Thanks to Yelland, Katherine Heath and the rest of a cast, just as energetic and appealing as that of 1983, the piece never succumbs to the silliness that would deprive it of tension. Oh yes, there's even a rousingly plausible school song by Beryl Waddle-Browne, who is ... well, anyone bad enough at verbal games not to deduce her identity should be tossed in a blanket in the dorm.

▷ In what ways does the reviewer see the play as 'a delightful comedy'?

▷ What do you learn about the central character, Daisy Meredith, from this review?

▷ What do you learn about the reviewer's own schooldays? Do you think he has made this up?

▷ What do comments like: 'I was fascinated . . . entranced . . . filled with nostalgia . . .' add to the review?

▷ What does he mean by, 'it makes a topping holiday from twenty-first century reality . . .'?

▷ Explain briefly, in your own words, what the reviewer thought of the play.

▷ How does his choice of language suit the play? Pick out some examples.

4 Now look at a very different review of three pop bands.

Pop
New to Q
*Shepherds Bush
Empire, W12*

★★☆☆☆

OASIS may be back sounding like the Beatles and bad-mouthing Blur, but don't expect a Britpop revival any time soon. The first date of a week of gigs hosted by *Q* magazine to showcase new talent boasted four indie acts, none of whom relied on Lennon and McCartney to come up with a tune. That said, some of the Gallaghers' showmanship would have been welcome.

The first band, Lorien, lived up to Coldplay comparisons with an enchanting set that mixed low-key lullabies like *Shivering Sun* with midtempo rockers such as former single *Ghostlost*, all from their recently released, debut album, *Under the Waves*. While it was full marks for the music, it was nul points for the performance. The part-English, part-Italian, part-Icelandic quartet barely moved a muscle and made no attempt to interact with the audience.

Athlete, from South London, were slightly more energetic, with the three of the four-piece (drummer excluded) nodding their heads David Gray-style to odd, electronic rock that made them sound like a moody XTC. All of Athlete's songs seemed to start off slow then quickly pick up speed, but it was only during the chaotic *Beautiful* that the band got the audience to groove along.

The singer with Manchester outfit Alfie had a more direct approach to crowd participation. He walked straight to the front of the stage and ordered everyone to clap their hands. Signed to the same indie label as Badly Drawn Boy, Alfie share Damon Gough's experimental approach to music-making. A line-up that went from five to eight people included cellist and harmonica, trumpet and saxophone players, while the shambolic songs mixed art-rock with funky rhythms. The most perplexing moment of the evening was Alfie's cover of Fat Larry's Band's *Zoom*, which began like a blissed-out tribute, but became a guitar-drenched joke.

It didn't help that it took 40 minutes for headliner Ed Harcourt to make it to the stage. At least the former Mercury Music Prize nominee made an effort when he got there. Wearing a black suit and bright red shirt with a collar so wide it made him look like Harry Hill, Harcourt almost attacked his little keyboard as he played, indulged in a spot of very bad dancing and told silly stories.

This was a one-off performance for the singer, who is completing the follow-up to last year's debut album *Here Be Monsters*. His set did include a few new tracks, mostly ballads, but it was jaunty, brass-backed favourites such as *Apple of My Eye* and *She Fell into My Arms* that the crowd wanted to hear. Harcourt not only obliged, but looked like he was enjoying it, something the less experienced bands on the bill would have done well to note.

Lisa Verrico

▶ Copy out the following table and write brief notes, under the two headings, about Lisa Verrico's comments on the bands.

NAME OF BAND	NEGATIVE COMMENTS	POSITIVE COMMENTS
Lorien		
Athlete		
Alfie		

▶ Using your completed grid to help you, comment on what Lisa Verrico seemed to think of the state of 'Britpop' bands in general?

▶ Would you like to go to a similar 'week of gigs hosted by *Q* magazine'? Why, or why not?

Part C: Writing to Comment

Every day, in almost every activity, we are *commenting* on something: what our five senses tell us, what other people are saying or doing, what we are or ought to be doing, and so on. Some of our comments can be frank to the point of bluntness or unkindness, others can be very subtle or diplomatic.

ROLE-PLAY

Role-play in pairs a situation which demands tact: you are going out for the evening with a friend and call round to their house to collect them. They are almost ready and invite you in. Then you notice something about their appearance (for example, an item of clothing or a new hairstyle), which is so awful you don't even want to be seen walking down the street with them! There isn't much time but you have to say *something*, without hurting their feelings too much.

Role-play your tactful comments to your friend. Then reverse roles with your partner. So, how did you keep your comments honest but not too unkind?

WRITING ACTIVITIES

1 Put what you have learned from the role-play exercise to good use: in playscript form, write the dialogue that might occur between a Headteacher and a parent, where the head has to explain a delicate matter about the pupil, for example, body odour, dandruff, suspected indecent graffiti writing, or substance abuse. You could begin like this:

HEADTEACHER: Good morning, Mrs Brown. Do sit down. Coffee?

MRS BROWN: Yes, thank you.

and build up to the point, showing how the Headteacher conducts the interview and how the parent responds.

2 Think of an occasion when something went wrong for you. Explain the situation and comment on what you learned from the experience later.

3 Write a letter to a cousin who is making his option choices in Year 9 and has asked you about what GCSEs are like. Comment on your experience of the work so far.

4 Read the following article on the banning of mobile phones in school. Write an article for a school newspaper in which you comment on the effect that mobile phones have had on your generation and whether or not they should be allowed in schools.

Mobile phones used to arrange school fight

A headteacher has banned pupils from bringing mobile phones to school – after they were used to arrange fights with pupils at another school.

Parents at Priestnall School in Stockport have been told that their children can no longer bring mobile phones into the classroom, after staff found that pupils were exchanging messages to set up fights.

The headteacher, Dr Graham Nelmes, has written to parents after text and voice messages had been passed between his pupils and those at Parrs Wood High in Didsbury, making arrangements for a fight.

Staff at Priestnall School have found that two-thirds of pupils are carrying mobile phones.

They will now only be allowed to bring them to school if they are needed for safety reasons – and will have to leave them in the school office during the day.

£5 fine for ringing in class

This is the latest attempt by a school to discourage the use of phones by its pupils – as an ever-increasing proportion of the school-age population acquires their own phone. Industry projections claim that 70% of young people under the age of 18 will have mobile phones by 2002.

Last week a school introduced fines to discourage the interruption of lessons by the ringing of mobile phones. Pupils at St Bartholomew's School in Newbury, Berkshire, are being fined £5 each time their phone rings in the classroom, because teachers have become fed up with interruptions.

Source: http://news.bbc.co.uk

5 Read the following plotted summary of the life of John Joseph Merlin, entitled 'Notable Blunders'. Using the article as a model, write a short newspaper article about someone whose actions have often been under public scrutiny, for example, Princess Diana or Christopher Columbus. Make sure that you put both points of view across before coming to your conclusion. You will need to carry out some research in order to find out the important events in his or her life.

NOTABLE
BLUNDERS

John Joseph Merlin's ingenious novelties

John Joseph Merlin proves that even the most successful people have very bad days. The man was a mechanical genius with an exhausting curriculum vitae. He made and played musical instruments, constructed fine clocks, built wheelchairs and robots, ran a museum, invented a barrel organ, and experimented with perpetual motion machines. But he still found time for socialising. In fact, John Joseph was a bit of a celebrity in 1770s London.

He lived on Oxford Street and moved with the smart set. He was mates with JC Bach (who played on his keyboards) and Thomas Gainsborough (who painted him).

Belgian by birth, Merlin had been persuaded to come to London as a technical adviser by the Spanish ambassador. People were having some difficulty understanding the chronometers invented by John Harrison of Longitude fame. Merlin did not have a lot of time for chronometers, but he clearly liked the city and decided to move there.

Just round the corner in Soho Square lived Mrs Corneily, a society hostess who invited the Belgian inventor to one of her celebrated masquerades.

Merlin got a bit carried away. He had recently come up with the idea of fixing small metal wheels on shoes. These first roller skates were of the inline variety (as was to be the case for the next 100 years), which made stopping or turning extremely difficult. Nevertheless, Merlin decided to wear his skates to Mrs C's do. He might have been all right ... had he not decided it would be fun to play the violin at the same time.

What happened was recorded in the newspapers. Merlin, wearing his 'ingenious novelties', 'impelled himself against a mirror of more than £500 value, dashed it to atoms, broke his instrument to pieces and wounded himself severely'.

He did not apply for a patent.

Stephanie Northen

TES TEACHER –
April 26 2002

66137330

60 2216

S ALPHE.